Wing Chun Kung-fu: A Complete Guide

VOLUME TWO

Fighting and Grappling

CHINESE MARTIAL ARTS LIBRARY

WING CHUN KUNG-FU

VOLUME TWO

Fighting & Grappling

Dr. Joseph Wayne Smith

CHARLES E. TUTTLE CO., INC.
Rutland, Vermont & Tokyo, Japan

Disclaimer

Please note that the publisher of this instructional book is
NOT RESPONSIBLE in any manner whatsoever for any injury that may result
from practicing the techniques and/or following the instructions given
within. Since the physical activities described herein may be too
strenuous in nature for some readers to engage in safely,
it is essential that a physician be consulted prior to training.

Published by the Charles E. Tuttle Publishing Co., Inc.
of Rutland, Vermont & Tokyo, Japan
with editorial offices at
1-2-6 Suido, Bunkyo-ku, Tokyo 112

LCC Card No. 92-80689
ISBN 0-8048-1719-7

First edition, 1992
Third printing, 1994

PRINTED IN SINGAPORE

Contents

Introduction

THE FIGHTING SKILLS OF WING CHUN KUNG-FU

This is the second volume in a three-volume treatise on the nature of Wing Chun kung-fu. The broad aim of these books is to present a concise, systematic, and scientific discussion of a somewhat controversial martial-art system. Chinese kung-fu, rightly or wrongly, has often been shrouded in secrecy and mysticism. There is often great vagueness about why skills are as they are, and why techniques work or do not work. Those who adopt a mystical approach to the martial arts are welcome to do so. But for those who do not accept that world view, these books may be what they are looking for. My approach to the martial arts is based upon common sense and an appreciation of biomechanical principles. However, this free thinking does not result in a freestyle approach where often incongruous techniques and approaches are thrown together in the hope of obtaining a coherent, complete, and unified combative art. What I have attempted to do here is to analyze a classical martial-arts system—Wing Chun kung-fu—using Western modes of thinking; namely, through examining it with logic, physics, and biomechanics, but without undue technicalities or the use of mathematics.

Volume one of this series gave a comprehensive analysis of the basic building blocks of the Wing Chun system, namely, the three forms—*Sil Lum Tao, Chum Kil,* and *Bil Jee.* The aim of that volume was to define terms, to outline the meaning of specific body movements, and to summarize the key principles of the Wing Chun system. That book was, to use a military metaphor, a study of martial-art *ballistics,* what the Wing Chun weapons are and how they work. This book is a study of martial-arts strategy, or *logistics,* or how to actually use the Wing Chun weapons in realistic combat situations. According to the scientific philosophy of the martial arts, the very point or reason for the existence of the martial arts is effective self-defense. Techniques must be judged by the criterion of whether they have worked or will work in a street situation for the average student, not whether the techniques are aesthetically elegant, beautiful, or graceful. There is a place for martial-arts aesthetics, but it is not in this system of Wing Chun kung-fu. Just as a scientist is concerned about whether or not a theory is predictively successful, I am concerned about whether or not a technique is combatively successful.

In volume one, an introduction to Wing Chun's *chi sao,* or sticky-hands, was given. This volume attempts to explain how to fight using the sticky-hands method. Sticky-hands is in bad need of a critical deconstruction or demystification, and this book attempts to do just that. Likewise, the Wing Chun method of sticky-leg, or *chi gerk,* fighting has been described in some instances as a way of sticking with one's legs to an opponent's kick. This is practically impossible to do for the average martial artist. Rather, a realistic theory of sticky-leg fighting is outlined, in which low kicks and sweeps are used in combination with grappling hand moves to destroy an opponent's equilibrium or to attack the joints. As far as this author is aware, this is the first time this type of *chi-gerk* fighting has been outlined in any detail in book form.

Attention is then given to the *chin-na* of Wing Chun. *Chin-na* means to seize *(chin)* and control *(na).* Wing Chun's *chin-na,* then, is a system of techniques for grasping, clawing, and tearing the flesh, skin, and muscles; spraining or breaking joints; attacking vital points of the human anatomy; and choking, strangling, and killing by breaking the neck in life-or-death situations. A discussion and illustration of clawing techniques, locking and throwing techniques, grappling and disabling throws, and vital strikes to the weak points of human anatomy are given. This is a vast area to cover, and no attempt is made to illustrate all such techniques. Rather, the emphasis here is upon basic techniques that you will be able to depend upon in a realistic self-defense situation, and the general principles of combat.

Finally, a critical analysis is given of the weakness of the Wing Chun system. The principal weakness of Wing Chun kung-fu lies next to its strengths: it is preoccupied with linear attacks and combat in a straight line as well as with close-range combat. Opponents would be likely to deal with the Wing Chun fighter by using either circular attacks or linear attacks delivered at a longer range, keeping the Wing Chun fighter at bay. Moreover, because of Wing Chun's preoccupation with both maintaining balance and close-range fighting, there is not enough emphasis placed upon fast footwork, relative to say Thai kick-boxing. The Wing Chun system is in need of enrichment. My proposal for Wing Chun's enrichment is as follows:

First, long-arm circular attacks, such as those found in White Crane kung-fu *(Pak Hok Kuen)* and many systems of karate, need to be added.

Second, Wing Chun needs to be practiced as a form of boxing without gloves, incorporating not only all the punches of Western boxing, but also all the kicks, knee attacks, and elbow attacks of Thai kick-boxing *(Muay Thai)*.

Third, Wing Chun proponents have never shown much interest in weight training. Contrary to the traditionalists, the author is a proponent of weight training in the martial arts, in particular, power training with heavy weights to maxime one's strength potential.

This approach to the martial arts is called *Sun Tzu Kuen*, after the great Chinese military thinker Sun Tzu. It offers the reader an advanced form of Wing Chun that deals with all of the objections critics from other styles have made about the art.

The knowledge contained in this volume will present the Wing Chun student, as well as the interested student of the martial arts in general, with a comprehensive and unified theory of combat.

1

Sticky-Hand Fighting (*chi sao*)

INTRODUCTION

Sticky-hand fighting (*chi sao*) is the foundation of the Wing Chun system. So important is this skill that the merits of a Wing Chun practitioner can be judged by his skill at sticky-hands alone. Yet many students of Wing Chun are confused about the meaning of *chi sao*; it is seen as no more than a training exercise, like shadow boxing, for developing, in this case, contact reflexes—the ability to spontaneously respond to an attack upon contact of the arms. This is true, but sticky-hands is much more than this—it is a way of fighting.

In this chapter, I shall explain how to fight using the sticky-hand techniques. I cannot in this guidebook show you every technique from the theory of sticky-hands, as that would take an entire book in itself. I can, however, discuss and illustrate the most basic and useful techniques, which I believe will give the reader an understanding of the fundamental principles behind *chi sao*, and this I feel is a more important task.

WHAT IS *CHI SAO*?

In fighting with the hands, an attack may be either evaded or else it is blocked or deflected. If it is blocked or deflected, then the attacker and the opponent's arm (typically, the forearms, or what is called the bridge) come into contact. *Chi sao* is a martial-art theory concerned with fighting at this instant. Instead of withdrawing and then counterattacking, as is usually done in Western boxing, in sticky-hands one clings or sticks to the opponent's forearms and attempts to penetrate his guard and thus secure a strike. There are many individual techniques designed for penetrating an opponent's guard once the forearms come into contact. In general, however, these moves may be classified into fundamental categories such as: trapping the arms; pushing the hands up or down, left or right; pulling the guard hand(s) down or clearing an entrance by the *jut sao;* forcing or grinding through the guard; twisting around or flicking a *bil jee* strike around the guard; and attacking under or over the bridge (e.g., using a *lap sao* technique—a *bong sao* with a rotating back fist).

Sticky-hand training has two parts. First, one finely tunes one's reflexes by two training drills known as single and double rolling hands. Both of these exercises are practiced in the parallel stance in order to train both hands equally. Second, one adds fighting techniques to the single and double sticky-hands techniques so that hand-free fighting can occur. At a more advanced level, sticky-leg techniques are added so that ultimately the student works up to performing sticky-hand and sticky-leg free sparring. In this section, I shall discuss the formal exercise of rolling hands; and in the next section, combat techniques.

Single *chi sao* is performed by two practitioners who face each other in the parallel stance. Person A forms a left or right *taun sao,* which person B locks up with a right or left *fook sao.* There is forward force (not downward force) on both of these hand moves, but not an exaggerated amount. In other words, you aim your weapon at your opponent, but do not push it through unless he is obviously open. This is so that you do not commit yourself to any particular direction and consequently create an opening for your opponent, who could then side-pivot, redirect your force, and strike.

From the *taun sao/fook sao* position, the person forming the *taun sao* performs a low palm-strike, careful not to draw his elbow into his own body. The other person destroys the force of the palm-strike with the wrist force of a *jut sao;* this person must be even more careful to maintain the fist-and-a-half distance between the elbow and the center-line, to lose it would be to simply draw the opponent's strike into his own body. The person who has done *jut sao* now punches toward his opponent's head. The opponent's arm sticks and rises into a defensive *bong sao*. Then both hands go back to the starting point of *taun sao/fook sao* and the sequence begins again. The practitioners swap hand moves on the *jut sao*/palm-strike position, the person doing the low palm-strike performs *haun sao* to get on the outside and punches up. The punch rises with a defensive *bong sao* and the sequence begins again. To change hands, one person punches with the previously stationary hand, which is met by a *bong sao* and the sequence continues. Single sticky-hands practice performed in this way, is a continuous flow of attack and defense.

Double *chi sao* is not the performance of single sticky-hands with both hands (although that would be a worthwhile exercise). Rather, the simple rolling exercise is as follows. Person A has either a *bong sao* or a *fook sao* with either his left or right hand, while person B has a punch or *taun sao* with the opposite hand. The rule is that at any time you have either: a) a *bong sao* and a *fook sao*, or b) a punch or a *taun sao*, then the *bong sao* always goes with the punch and the *taun sao* and *fook sao* go together. If person A is in the *bong sao/fook sao* position, then he rotates to *taun sao*/punch and person B does the corresponding move. To change hands, one performs *haun sao* and punches from the inner hand (the hand inside the opponent's guard), which is met with *bong sao*, and the opponent does the same. Then simply drop down into *taun sao/fook sao* on the opposite side and start rotating again.

The most important aspect of either of these exercises is to develop a good defense of the center-line (median axis of the body) by getting the elbow in the center-line. A sticky-hands performance with the elbow out of the center-line, particularly one in which the hands sway from side to side like palm trees in a storm is extremely poor because this sort of rotation is wide open to a strike from either the *taun sao* (the inner hand) or the *fook sao* (the other hand). To develop a good center-line defense, or a so-called good elbow, some hard training is necessary. First, one must stretch the chest muscles and shoulder muscles (especially the lateral deltoids). Second, sticky-hands must be performed using the cane-circle hand. The idea here is to force the upper arms (not the forearms as some students believe) together with a round of cane, or even a piece of cloth. Sticky-hands is then performed. As the elbow improves, a cane circle with a smaller diameter can be used. This advice is an illustration of the profound simplicity of Wing Chun: its best skills and training methods make one think, "Of course, why didn't I think of that!" It is easy then to see why so much of Wing Chun kung-fu has been veiled in secrecy for so long.

STICKY-HAND FIGHTING SKILLS

1. BASIC HAND TRAP

The idea behind hand trapping is to use one of your hands to cut an opponent's arm down upon his other arm, so that it is pressed upon his body and is momentarily dead. This situation occurs when one of your hands is on top of your opponent's hand. At that instant, an opening for a strike to the head exists. Repeated hits can be performed while maintaining the trap by alternating the hands that respectively hold and punch.

Another form of trapping hands involves using the opponent's own body to cut off his attack. This occurs when the attacker gets into an opponent's side and, with one of his arms, locks up the opponent's upper arm, forcing it onto the opponent's chest. Once again, a clear shot at the face is possible, and again, repeated hits involve maintaining the trap and alternating the hands that respectively hold and punch.

The cut-and-punch trap can be countered by moving your bottom hand out of the cut and using the internal close-body *taun sao*, deflecting the punch and immediately counter-attacking. The side trap must be evaded by footwork, moving to release the pressure on the upper arm, parrying the pressing arm, and countering with a *bil jee*, back fist, or side hammer-punch.

2. ONE-STEP GUARD-CLEARING TECHNIQUES

There are a number of techniques in sticky-hand fighting that are called one-step guard-clearing techniques. Typically, these techniques involve one deflection or angle-altering hand move, with a follow-up attack. The *taun sao* and punch/palm-strike is the simplest of these.

From a *taun sao* with the inside hand, turn out the opponent's outer hand, and strike through the opening. Or alternatively, perform this move, but fake a strike, and attack instead with the opposite hand. Another good technique is to alter the angles of the opponent's defense, so that an opening materializes. For example, in the rolling hands, when you rotate from *bong sao/fook sao* to *taun sao*/punch, with your left hand in *bong sao*, try applying a slight circular force to the motion forming the *taun sao* so that your opponent's hands both move to the left. At that split second, a free path opens up for an attack.

Apart from these techniques, there are many other one-step guard-clearing techniques. You may push a hand out of the way or lift it up; a hand may be cleared by the downward force of the *jut sao*, or a *bil jee* strike may be forced through using the piercing-hands technique from the *Chum Kil* form. The opponent's hands may also be drawn downward, so that they come together (constituting a partial trap) and a strike made through the opening to the hand which is then created.

3. ROTATIONAL FORCE

The Wing Chun fighter's hand must be flexible like a snake, one of the animals that is used to symbolically represent the system. Many sticky-hand skills are based upon rotation of the wrist or elbow to secure strikes. You may, for example, by *haun sao* or wrist twisting, get both of your hands on the superior inside position and force the opponent's arms out of his center-line, attacking with a double palm strike. Again, if your hand is on the outside position, you may rotate your hand inside the opponent's center-line and flick your fingers into his face. Another excellent skill from the *Bil Jee* form is to rotate an arm that is on the inside of an opponent's upheld arm, cutting down with a palm strike or hammer punch into the opponent's face.

4. GRAB-AND-CHOP TECHNIQUE

The grab-and-chop technique is an excellent skill that can be devastating in combat. The idea of this technique is to grab the opponent's hand under the bridge (forearm) of your *bong sao* and launch a chop to the throat. This chop is usually blocked by the opponent with a *taun sao*. However, you can then grab the *taun sao* and pull and chop above it, pulling the opponent down at a 45-degree angle. This second chop will be successful because the opponent's balance is destroyed as he is forced to trip over himself. This skill is used extensively in Wing Chun's *chin-na,* which is discussed below.

5. PULLING AND PUSHING FORCES

Wing Chun's sticky-hand fighting makes extensive use of pulling and pushing actions to clear away defenses and to render defenses ineffective. The simplest way in which this can be done is by lifting the opponent's arms up and attacking under the bridge. Another technique involves parrying the opponent's *taun sao* from your *bong sao,* and slipping an uppercut (lifting punch) under the bridge and through the guard to the head. A subtle use of pushing force is the tracing-the-shape palm, found in the *Bil Jee* form of some forms of Wing Chun, which I discussed previously in the *Bil Jee* chapter in volume one. This technique is used to control the upper arms of the opponent, clinging to them and forcing them onto the opponent's own body so that his arms are momentarily trapped and you are free to strike his face.

Pushing force is a neglected aspect of contemporary martial-arts training, only being adequately developed by the Japanese in sumo wrestling and surprisingly enough by the Americans in American football, and by the Australians in "Aussie Rules" football. The push, however, is an excellent balance-destroying technique. In Wing Chun training, students train both shoulders and hips in pushing techniques that illustrate a broader principle, namely that students should aim to mold their entire bodies into weapons—not merely their hands and legs.

An example of the use of pulling force comes from the *Bil Jee* form (previously mentioned). Another method of clearing a guard is to pull at the opponent's defensive hand, not to disrupt his balance, but to alter the angle of the defensive hand so that the way is cleared for a punch. For example, against your straight punch, the opponent defends with a *bong sao.* You grasp the opponent's hand with your free hand, and pull so that the *bong sao* straightens out and your punch sails right over the top of the *bong sao.*

I have summarized here some of the fundamental sticky-hand

techniques. While many of the more complex techniques have not been discussed or illustrated here, the above outline does, I believe, give the reader a useful guide to sticky-hand fighting. But that is not all there is to Wing Chun combat. As well as sticky-hand fighting, there is also sticky-leg fighting and *chin-na*. These skills must be added to the foundation that has already been constructed.

1

2

3

STICKY-HAND FIGHTING TECHNIQUES

1. This illustrates the start position of the single sticky-hands training drill. The larger fighter on the left delivers a left-hand *taun sao*, which is locked up by the smaller fighter's right *fook sao*. Notice that the elbows, and not merely the wrists, are aligned along the center-line.

2. The larger fighter delivers a palm-strike from the *taun sao* position toward his opponent's groin. The smaller fighter deflects this attack with a *jut sao* or downward-deflecting palm-strike. Because the hands are in contact, the attack is felt and the hands stick to each other, or follow each other's force.

3. From this previous position the smaller fighter has a strategic advantage, because his hand is on top of his opponent's hand, effectively controlling it. Therefore he punches toward the larger fighter's head. However, the larger fighter again feels this attack

4   5

coming because of the upward release of pressure and rises up, sticking to the punch to deflect it with a *bong sao*. The larger fighter then drops his left arm from the *bong sao* to the *taun sao* position, while the smaller fighter sticks on all the time locking up the arm. The sequence is completed by returning to the *taun sao/fook sao* position. The sequence is then repeated.

This drill is repeated on the opposite side by either proponent punching, the other proponent deflecting the punch with a *bong sao*, and the sequence continues. The point of this drill is to train fluid and fast combinations of basic hand moves and contact sensitivity—to respond to an attack by feeling alone. For this reason, *chi sao* is often practiced blindfolded.

4. This is the start position for the double sticky-hands rotation drill. The larger fighter's left arm is in the *bong sao* formation. It is sticking to the smaller fighter's right punch. The larger fighter's right arm is in the *fook sao* formation. It is locking up the smaller fighter's left *taun sao*. This exercise combines the movements that we saw previously in the single sticky-hand drill.

5. Now rotate your arms. This is done by the larger fighter forming a left *taun sao*, which the smaller fighter locks up with a right *fook sao*. The larger fighter's right punch is locked up by the smaller fighter's left *bong sao*. Then return to the start position. To do this, the smaller fighter forms simultaneously a left *taun sao* and right punch, to which the larger fighter responds with a left *bong sao* and right *fook sao*, respectively. The double sticky-hands rotation drill may now be continued. This exercise symbolizes a hands-on combat situation.

6   7

8   9

6. Attack and defense skills can be added to the basic double sticky-hands rotation drill. From the start position shown in Figure 4, the smaller fighter may cut down the larger fighter's *bong sao* onto his other arm, so that a hand-trap is formed. Notice how the larger fighter's top arm is pressed down onto his lower arm.

7. From this position, the smaller fighter withdraws his bottom arm, which was locking up (from below) his opponent's arms. The trap is still maintained by pushing down the larger fighter's crossed arms. This allows a clear punch to the chin to be delivered.

8. This attack can be countered by the larger fighter quickly withdrawing his bottom arm in a windshield-wiper-type motion (in this case the right arm) from the arm trap, and using a *taun sao* to deflect the punch off the center-line.

9. The larger fighter then immediately follows through with a cutting side-palm to the smaller fighter's nose, which is illustrated here.

10   11

12   13

10. The smaller fighter could defend against the previous palm-strike by pivoting his body slightly on the spot, or even by turning his body to the side, simultaneously chopping down with his forearm on the in-coming palm-strike, deflecting it.

11. Now, from this position, the smaller fighter grabs the larger fighter's former attacking arm, jerks it down, and then delivers a punch to the chin.

12. In turn, the larger fighter may again defend against this attack by deflecting the smaller fighter's punch with a *taun sao*.

13. The larger fighter may then counter-attack with a palm-strike. This sequence of photographs illustrates the *continuous* nature of the Wing Chun attack and defense in sticky-hand fighting.

14. The larger fighter's palm-strike can be countered by the smaller fighter in a fashion that we have already seen—pivot counterclockwise to the left 90 degrees and cut down the incoming attack.

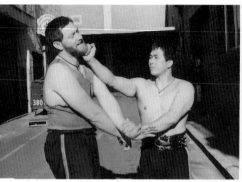

14   15

16   17

Then maintain a hand-trap, as we have already seen, and deliver a
counter-attack in the form of a punch to the larger fighter's chin.

15. Once again there is a way for the larger fighter to defeat this
attack before he is punched. As soon as his hands are forced
downward, the larger fighter simply pivots his body clockwise 90
degrees, or at least twists his trunk to one side to counter the
downward force. It is therefore possible now to raise the once
trapped arm upward to form a *bong sao* to defend against the smaller
fighter's punch.

16. Now a counter-attack can be launched. The larger fighter
pivots to the front from the side position, simultaneously lifting his
bong sao. Notice how the smaller fighter has grabbed the *bong sao* to
prepare for yet another attack. Here, however, the force of the pivot
and the lifting motion of the larger fighter's arm is sufficient to raise
both of the smaller fighter's arms. In doing so, an opening is created,
and the larger fighter proceeds to deliver a punch to the chin
through the created opening.

17. However, the smaller fighter instantly responds to this attack

18

19

20

21

by pulling down the larger fighter's *bong sao*. The smaller fighter's arm, which was previously forced, seemingly helplessly, into the air, is now smashed down in a hammer-punch to the collarbone.

18. Suppose now, somewhat optimistically, that the hammer punch is deflected by the larger fighter's right parry in a fashion that we have already seen. This will lead us to the combat situation depicted in this photograph, illustrating an elementary *chin-na* technique. The larger fighter has caught the smaller fighter in an arm-bar and is just about to break the arm at the elbow joint.

19. However, before the arm-bar can be applied, the smaller fighter counters this technique by quickly bending his arm.

20. The larger fighter immediately abandons the failed arm-bar and delivers a palm-strike to the face.

21. The smaller fighter counters this palm-strike in a fashion already seen, by pivoting clockwise away from the strike, and parrying the palm-strike down so that the larger fighter's arms can be trapped once more. Then the smaller fighter delivers a punch to the head.

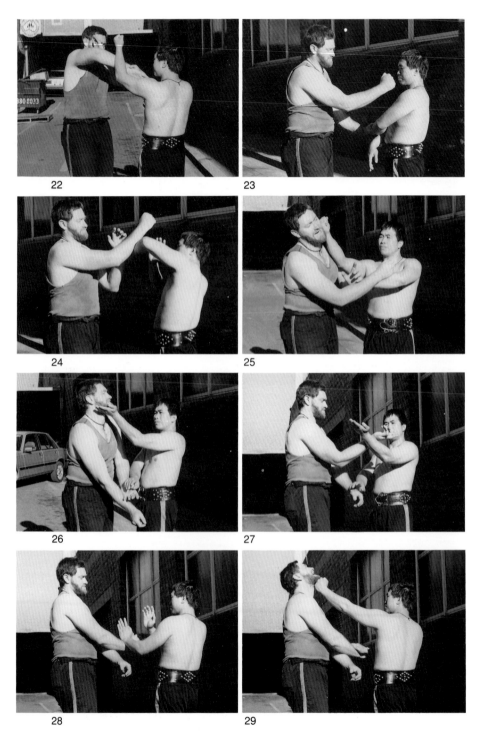

22

23

24

25

26

27

28

29

30   31

22. The larger fighter is once more in a seemingly desperate position. However, using his superior strength and perhaps with luck on his side, he manages to defeat the hand-trap and deflect the smaller fighter's punch with a *bong sao*. Notice the larger fighter's left hand: it is held behind the *bong sao* in a guard position.

23. This behind-the-*bong-sao* guard sweeps the smaller fighter's arm down, trapping both arms. Then, from the *bong sao*, a punch is delivered.

24. However, the smaller fighter is also able to counter this punch with a *bong sao* by instantly snapping up his arms the moment the larger fighter had finished cutting down.

25. The smaller fighter, seeing that the larger fighter's rear guard is defective because it is too close to his other attacking arm sees an opening on the side. The smaller fighter pivots and delivers a back-fist to the ear. (The back-fist moves in a high-to-low fashion, using the back of the two largest knuckles to strike, with a whiplike snap on impact.)

26. The smaller fighter's right arm then cuts down, trapping the larger fighter's arms. The smaller fighter then responds with a chop to the throat.

27. Though dazed from the back fist, the larger fighter is, however, able to stop the chop with a *taun sao*, and being in the center-line prepares to counterattack with a chop to the nose.

28. The smaller fighter immediately counters, by chopping down the larger fighter's *taun sao*, once again trapping his hands.

29. The smaller fighter then attacks with a punch.

30. Again, this attack is defeated by the larger man's inner *taun sao*, which, as can be seen, deflects his opponent's punch.

31. In the by-now familiar fashion, the larger fighter applies a hand-trap by again cutting down the smaller fighter's arm.

32   33   34

35

32. Having applied the trap, the larger fighter delivers another punch to the smaller fighter's jaw.

33. This punch is, however, countered by the smaller fighter's *taun sao*.

34. From the *taun sao*, the smaller fighter delivers a powerful side palm-strike to the larger fighter's jaw.

35. The larger fighter is now defeated. Dazed again by the palm-strike, his arms are caught in an arm-bar, as we have seen previously. His arm is now broken at the elbow joint. To illustrate this, the arm positions have been reversed in these photographs.

2

Sticky-Leg Fighting (*chi gerk*)

THEORETICAL CONSIDERATIONS

Sticky-leg fighting *(chi gerk)* is the jewel of the Wing Chun system. The *chi gerk* techniques are extremely easy to learn and highly effective in close-range combat. In this chapter, I shall give you a concise summary of the nature of sticky-leg fighting and teach you how to train to improve your skills in this mode of combat.

First, I would like to describe what Wing Chun's sticky-leg techniques—as I view them—are not. They are not strictly analogous to sticky-hand techniques, in that you don't try to stick to kicks in mid-air (try this and see how absurd this idea really is), nor do you trap an opponent's legs as you do his hands, by somehow crossing them together. The former view is inconsistent with the Wing Chun fighter's passion for balance, "the root of the tree," while the latter position is not a practical skill as the reader may verify by personal experimentation. What then is sticky-leg fighting?

Sticky-leg fighting is concerned with attacking the foundation of the opponent's offense and defense: his legs. There are two fundamental and interrelated ways in which this can be done in close-range fighting. The first is by destroying the opponent's equilibrium. The second is by directly attacking the knee joint or the lower leg. The result of both types of attacks is the same: the foundation or basis of both the opponent's offense and defense is lost, and if a broken knee doesn't stop him you are at full liberty to use any number of other techniques to put his lights out.

Let us first consider the nature of attacks on the equilibrium or balance in sticky-leg fighting. An attack on an opponent's equilibrium might involve locking up his leg and while launching a hand attack, simultaneously pulling one of his legs out from under him, using your own leg as a hook. When this is done, your own attacking leg must not be raised off the ground, as is stressed by Wing Chun's walking theory. This is to maintain your own balance while attacking an opponent's balance, because: first, it takes relatively little time to transfer body weight from one foot (which will be raised only long enough to effect a kick or hook) to the other (which will stay on the ground), and second, keeping both feet on the ground increases the size of your base of support, thus constituting greater stability than motion where one foot is held completely off the ground. In summary, sticky-leg fighting skills are characterized by a concern with stability. Consequently, kicks are predominantly aimed below the knee, although the knee itself is particularly vulnerable to sticky-leg attacks.

The leg-pulling technique is often combined with arm pulling. The idea is to lock up an opponent's leg, pull it with your own leg, and then to jerk his arm so that he falls. If the opponent's leg sticks to yours and moves with you as the gap between his knees widens, your attacking foot may slice into the testicles with the blade of the foot. Alternatively the knee of the opponent's other foot, which is now supporting the opponent's body weight, can be attacked. It is not generally realized, but two of the kicks from the *Chum Kil* form have a direct application in sticky-leg fighting. The ball-of-the-foot lifting kick can be used against an opponent who charges into you so that he runs into your foot, but it can also be used to attack the groin in sticky-leg fighting by lifting into the testicles when a leg is pulled open. The side-footage kick can be used as a defense against a roundhouse kick; it is also a first-class means of attacking the groin by slicing the blade of the foot into the testicles.

The opponent's equilibrium can be destroyed by low leg kicks. The *til toi* kick involves drag-kicking the back foot, with the toes raised to tense the front calf muscle, to strike against the soft calf muscle of the opponent's leg. This powerful kick, which uses the shin as a striking surface, when combined with hand techniques, can take down an opponent or completely numb his lower leg, preventing him from initiating further kick attacks against you.

A *par toi* kick uses the bottom of the foot (especially the heel if shoes are worn) to either uproot an opponent by kicking his legs out from under him or to break or injure his lower leg, especially the ankle. If an opponent is not wearing strong shoes, or has bare feet, it is highly effective to kick the instep, ankle, or toes, forcefully. If you are wearing strong-soled shoes, another good technique is to scrape the edge of your shoes against his shin, or to stamp with full power on his toes in order to destroy his kicking ability.

Finally, the circling-foot technique from the *Bil Jee* form also serves the dual purpose of uprooting the opponent and injuring his leg—this time the back of the heel is used to numb the calf muscle or back of the ankle. It is surprising how much pain can be rendered from this sort of attack.

The most sophisticated sticky-leg techniques center around attacking and breaking the opponent's leg at the knee joint. One simple way of numbing the leg is this: when you attempt to lock up your opponent's leg, charge into him, slamming your bent knee into the soft connective tissue at the side of his knee. The resulting instant of sharp pain may give you that split second needed to apply some finishing technique. In any case, this sort of jarring ill-treatment will take its toll on your opponent's legs, severely weakening his kicks, ultimately softening him up for other techniques.

A skilled sticky-leg fighter can charge into an opponent, lock up his leg, straighten it using his own leg as a lever, and then, like a powerful clamp or vice, snap the opponent's leg at the knee. This is done by falling or thrusting forward with your full weight onto the knee joint.

Another way of producing a serious injury is to lock up the opponent's leg, straighten it, and then violently jerk him forward so that his body is jerked against his own knee joint. This will also produce a severe break. With a broken leg, your opponent is virtually helpless—if he is not crippled with pain, then his effectiveness in fighting has been nullified, because he can no longer attack with any effective footwork and has lost his foundation for the execution of powerful fighting techniques.

What are the defenses against sticky-leg attacks? The wrong thing to do, unless you are of superior strength, is to resist the pulling. It is more effective to move with the pull, to flow with, rather than against, this force. You may then add to the opponent's force by pushing him with your hands in the same direction in which he is pulling you, or you may initiate a pull of your own. Counter attempts to straighten and break your knee by keeping your knee bent. Again, flow with the force rather than resisting his leg attack head-on. There are a number of options against this attack: (1) you could move around your opponent and try to break the side of his knee; (2) you could move away from his attacking leg and attack his own supporting leg.

We also need to consider how to defend against very low kicks. These low kicks are extremely fast and powerful, and there is no conceivable way in which you can flow with the force of these kicks. The only options open to you are to make sure that your footwork is fast and fluid, that you move before he kicks you, and that you stick to and control his legs at the first chance. This recommendation is not banal or trivial: it takes a lot of practice to become proficient at sticking to an opponent who may attempt to run in order to set up a favorable kicking range. Furthermore, if you keep your opponent busy with your own attacks, he is not going to have much time to mount a strong kicking offensive of his own. Therefore, be fast, aggressive, and get a destructive attack in first—but, above all, be careful!

TRAINING FOR STICKY-LEG TECHNIQUES

The skills outlined above, as I have said, are very simple and easy to learn, taking only about one lesson to explain. The truly difficult part is training to perfect these techniques. In this section I detail some ways of training to help you perfect your skills in sticky-leg fighting.

First, sticky-leg fighting is greatly aided by the development of strong leg muscles, especially the muscles of the lower thigh and the front of the calf. Standard weight-lifting exercises, such as the full squat, leg extensions, and leg curls, along with front and back calf raises, are good exercises for overall development of leg strength.

In addition to these exercises, it is important to develop the capacity to pull weights with your foot. In the old days a tree was tied to the ankle, and the resistance of the tree to bending provided progressive resistance. Another more modern way to develop pulling power is to use a weight stack with a low cable and a leather foot loop. The advantage of the modern equipment is the very strong resistance that is offered, as additional weight can always be added to the stack. An isometric exercise involving pulling can be performed by hooking one's leg to a fixed object, such as a steel pole and pulling. The pole can also be used to train the leg-straightening and leg-breaking skills.

It is also necessary to train one's defenses against sticky-leg techniques. A good way of doing this is to have an opponent try to pull your leg out from under you by using his hands, while you resist by gripping the floor with your toes. You can also train against two partners, who lock up both of your legs and attempt to pull you over.

To develop power in the low kicks of the sticky-leg skill, train on a lowly-strung heavy bag. Serious students may consider toughening their shins as Thai kick-boxers do, by progressive abrasion—kicking sand bags, gravel bags, and bags of gun slugs—as was discussed in volume one.

Sticky-leg fighting is often used in conjunction with the sticky-hand techniques previously described. The theory here is not only to simultaneously attack an opponent and defend against counterattacks with your hands, but also to simultaneously attack the opponent's legs and his balance. To use two hands and one leg simultaneously is difficult and it requires dedicated practice to master this skill. This is Wing Chun fighting at its best, and it is the level to which all serious students should strive. At a minimum, the basic sticky-leg techniques that I have described here—and which, I believe, were first described in Western martial-art literature in an article jointly written by me and Sifu Leong ["Futshan Pai Wing Chun: China's Best-kept Secret," *Inside Kung Fu* 14(5): 80—83, 104 (May 1987)] will serve you well.

36   37   38

STICKY-LEG FIGHTING TECHNIQUES

36. This sequence of photographs illustrates Wing Chun leg attacks, sticky-leg or *chi gerk,* fighting. As these attacks are combined with the sticky-hand attacks previously analyzed and illustrated, this sequence of photographs will illustrate Wing Chun leg attacks in the context of hands-on combat. In this photograph, you can see the trademark of Wing Chun kicking. The larger fighter's knee is attacked by a knee kick, or by placing the foot on the knee and simultaneously stepping down through the knee while jerking the opponent forward so that his body whip-lashes over his own knee, thereby breaking or severly injuring it.

37. The *par toi* kick illustrated here is used to sweep the foot, but is also frequently used as a painful ankle attack—especially by using the heel of one's shoe to smash an opponent's ankle or to scrape the skin off the ankle.

38. In a combat situation like that depicted here, sticky-leg techniques often involve stepping down on, or falling through the opponent's knee joint, using one's falling body weight to attack the knee joint.

> **Note: These are self-defense techniques and caution must be exercised in any training situation. The human knee is surprisingly easy to dislocate and its correction may require surgery.**

39   40

                    41   42

39. Wing Chun kicks are seldom delivered higher than the groin. Here, a heel-kick is delivered to the testicles, crushing them against the pelvic bone.

40. Here, the *til toi* kick is used as a sweep, or to numb the opponent's calf muscle. The striking area is the shin.

41. After delivering the *til toi* kick, it is natural to unbalance an opponent by leg hooking and lifting as shown here, so as to keep the opponent off balance. This lack of balance destroys both his offense and defense.

42. The lifting technique can be combined with arm attacks. Here, it can be used with a powerful elbow smash to the throat.

43

44

45

46

43. Again, it can be combined with an arm trap and coordinated with a punch or back-fist to the face, so that the forces of both the punch and the lift simultaneously tip the opponent backward.

44. The same principle can be used in the arm-bar technique that I reviewed previously. The difference here is that when the opponent falls backward, his arm is still held, so that as he falls backward he breaks his own elbow.

45. This skill can also be used to attack the rear supporting leg, which as seen here, supports the opponent's entire body weight. The attacker would step down on the side of the knee joint to cause a severe break or tear of tendons and ligaments.

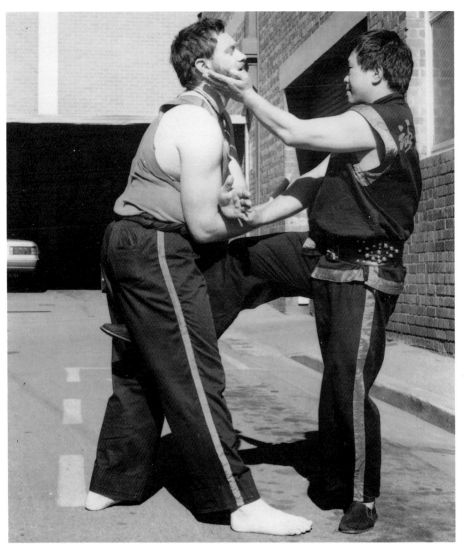

47

46. The knee can also be locked up and straightened and the knee joint put under pressure as illustrated here. This (obviously enough) prevents a retreat, and can also be used to attack and injure the knee joints.

47. The leg may also be pulled out and a shin-kick delivered to the testicles. As illustrated by all of these photographs, in Wing Chun, it is important to not only simultaneously defend and attack, but to do so with both legs and arms.

3

Grappling and Throwing Techniques (*chin-na*)

INTRODUCTION

Chin-na means to seize *(chin)* and control *(na)*. Wing Chun's *chin-na*, as I view it, is a system of techniques for grasping, clawing, and tearing the flesh, skin, and muscles; spraining or breaking joints; attacking vital points of the human anatomy; and choking, strangling, and killing by breaking the neck in life-or-death situations. If *chin-na* attacks are adequately performed, with both speed and power, counterattacks are difficult—especially against the Wing Chun fighter who attempts to fight from the side or behind. The idea is to use the *chin-na* in such a fashion that the opponent is paralyzed with pain and cannot fight back. In desperate situations, such as a vicious rape attack, techniques include gouging the eyes out of their sockets, dislocating the jaw, tearing at the ears and lips, and crushing the testicles.

Wing Chun's *chin-na* consists of three sections. The first section, which I shall now discuss, is the use of the claw-hand in grappling.

THE WING CHUN CLAW-HAND

The claw-hand is first seen in the beginning of the *Sil Lum Tao* level of Wing Chun, but its successful application requires a knowledge of the poison-touch strikes *(dar mak)* to vital points of human anatomy, which I shall discuss a little later. For the moment, I wish to describe the claw-hand.

The claw-hand of Wing Chun kung-fu is exactly like the claw of Eagle Claw kung-fu (*Ying Jow Pai*), although it is often performed incorrectly with the fingers open. This type of claw, known as a tiger claw, has its principal use in raking the face and eyes, but it is too weak for tearing the flesh. Wing Chun's claw has all of the fingers together, with the second knuckles bent to form semi-circles when viewed edge-on.

Training of the Wing Chun claw-hand requires both a flexible wrist and strong and powerful fingers. Both of these requirements are met in the basic training of Wing Chun. Wrist flexibility is developed at the *Sil Lum Tao* level and put into combat use in *chi sao*. Finger strength and conditioning, as we have seen, is developed at the *Bil Jee* level. Wing Chun's *chin-na* is an extension of this training.

Against a straight punch, we would either evade the punch or deflect it, and simultaneously counterattack with a hand technique to an opponent's vital point—such as the throat—as well as catch the opponent's arm in a claw, twisting strongly conditioned fingertips into the nerve center of the inner elbow. While doing this, care is taken to attack the opponent on a side angle, locking up his leg and jamming or trapping his arms using *chi sao* techniques.

Wing Chun *chin-na* gives us a simple, general, and unified way of countering many throws, locks, and chokes. There are, of course, many Wing Chun techniques designed to break locks—such as the *haun sao* (to twist or lever one's hand out of the lock), the *jut sao* (to cut against the opponent's thumb while twisting out of a lock), and the double low *bong sao* from the *Chum Kil* form (especially designed to deal with a bear hug by stepping forward and thrusting down to break the grip). However, throws, locks, and chokes depend upon an opponent's getting a grip on your body or clothing. The throwing techniques of Judo are a good illustration of this. Now, if this is so, then it seems logical that the best attack to make against an opponent who is trying to throw you is to attack the weak point of the throw: the grip. If an opponent has no firm grip on you, then the only way in which he can put you on the floor is by either knocking you out with a kick or punch or by sweeping your feet—in which case he ceases to be a grappler and can be dealt with by hand and leg attacks.

Escapes from locks and chokes such as the single winglock, cross strangle, full nelson, and various headlocks can be aided by *chin-na*. You will find that either you have one hand free, or you can work at getting one hand free by twisting and rolling. Again, attack the weak point of the lock—the fingers—which can be given various degrees of pain by twisting, including being systematically broken. Strikes or gouges against the nerve centers of your opponent's arm and/or hands are also effective in securing release, including pinching and grasping folds of skin or muscle and tearing.

If an opponent has taken you to the ground and is attempting various leg locks, such as the figure-4 leg lock, attack his groin or claw his eyes. Obviously, this sort of fighting cannot be used in sports competition, as it is devised to be lethal for desperate moments in street fighting. As such, clawing techniques offer women the best method of defending themselves in rape attacks. The rape attack of necessity must take place at close range, and especially if the opponent attacks you by surprise, or in the dark, there can be no chance for fancy kicks and punches. Furthermore, with the popularity of martial arts nowadays, it is quite possible that a potential rapist may be a trained martial artist, well prepared for your classic knee attack to the groin. To defend against rape requires extremely dirty fighting, which I believe is morally justified under the circumstances. Use deception to go along with the act; lovingly caress his face and then gouge out both of his eyes—or alternatively twist and crush and rip at his sex organ, even tearing away the testicles. This style of fighting does not require great skill and long hard years of practice—all it requires is courage and determination.

In conclusion, a claw-hand that is well conditioned and powerful can deliver instant crippling pain to an opponent. Surprisingly enough, a powerful claw-hand is all that is needed to break virtually any wrestling lock, providing of course you attack before the grappler breaks your arm or neck!

LOCKING AND THROWING TECHNIQUES: GENERAL PRINCIPLES

I have discussed the use of the claw-hand in Wing Chun *chin-na;* this skill is however only a small part of the total subject of *chin-na*, which is also concerned with locking techniques or wrestling holds and throws or takedowns.

A wrestling hold may be defined as a technique that involves holding an opponent so as to: 1) force a body part in a direction to which it does not naturally move, causing damage to a joint or the limbs, trunk, neck, or head (e.g., arm bar, elbow crank); 2) stretch muscles beyond the limits of their flexibility (e.g., groin stretch); or 3) to apply pressure to the trunk or the throat (e.g., bear hug, stranglehold). A throw or a takedown may be defined as a technique that puts an opponent either on the ground, or substantially disrupts his balance. Without doubt, the major advantage of correctly executed locks and throws is that they can render vulnerable foes who would be difficult to beat into submission by punches and kicks. Surprisingly enough, in contests between top-class wrestlers and Western boxers, the wrestlers usually come out on top. (*See* M. Griffin, *Fall Guys* [Chicago: Reilly and Lee Co., 1937], pp. 27–28.)

Locking and throwing techniques are perhaps best known to the reader from pro-wrestling or TV wrestling. Throwing in this great drama typically involves the use of sheer brute strength (and cooperation!), typically employing the body slam where an opponent is picked up and slammed so that he cannot break his fall. Many colorful locks are also employed such as the figure-4 leg-locks, the Boston crab, the Indian death-lock, and the head scissors. While the execution of these techniques provides good entertainment, they are too impractical to use on the street and require great strength and acting ability. (For more on pro-wrestling, see G.P. Stone, "Wrestling: The Great American Passion Play," in: E. Dunning, ed., *The Sociology of Sport: A Selection of Readings,* [London: Frank Cass, 1971], pp. 301–355.) In Wing Chun only very simple locks are employed, and at that only those locks that can attack the weakest joints. In this section, I shall outline the safest grappling techniques to use against an opponent who may counterattack with a kick or a punch rather than with a counter-hold.

Amateur wrestling takedowns include: 1) leg takedowns; 2) ducking under an opponent's arm and lifting the body; 3) dragging him by an arm and spinning him to get around him; and 4) twisting the torso. Leg takedowns might involve double leg takedowns such as gripping the thighs and lifting or single leg lifts. (*See* J. Rabel and R. Preobrazenski, "Wrestling Strategy: Tie-up Effectiveness for

Takedowns," *Canadian Journal of Applied Sport Sciences* 3:147–52 [1978], and B. Douglas, *Wrestling: The Takedown* [Ithaca, NY: Cornell University Press, 1972].) Again, this style of fighting is alien to Wing Chun because there are real dangers of being struck while ducking to grab a limb. Wing Chun's takedowns and throws are few in number because of the need to defend against an opponent's counter strikes. Wing Chun does not, for example, use the *tai otoshi*-style techniques of judo, the basic drop-throw, as it involves turning your back to an opponent, and Wing Chun views this as a vulnerability because a foe may punch you or claw you before you can throw him. Indeed, Wing Chun's throwing techniques are totally unlike judo's. Wing Chun fighters have little interest in merely throwing someone to the ground, because a person skilled in *ukemi*, the art of falling, can usually break his fall and rise uninjured, unless he falls on something dangerous, such as a broken bottle. In Wing Chun, the reason for throwing an opponent is not just to use the throw but to injure the opponent, using the momentum of the throw to break a limb. Throwing skills are therefore for offensive self-defense rather than for sport. Furthermore, Wing Chun combines wrestling locks and throws in a unique fighting methodology.

Before detailing these skills, it is well worthwhile to summarize some of the theory behind *chin-na*, namely the physics of leverage and balance. Wing Chun *chin-na* is not a hard art, it is a soft art employing mechanical advantage to defeat a foe.

Let us begin by looking at the idea of leverage. The human body itself is a system of levers—we can move because the bones of the body act as levers that are acted upon by the force produced by the contraction of muscles. Levers are mechanical devices used to produce turning motion about an axis. A lever consists of a fulcrum or axis of rotation, a power arm which is the distance from the fulcrum to the point where the force is applied, and a weight arm which is the distance from the fulcrum to the weight upon which the force is acting. Levers are of use to us because of the principle of mechanical advantage. The mechanical advantage of a lever is represented by the ratio of the length of the force or power arm, to the weight arm. The longer the force arm, the greater the moment of force about the axis. The shorter the force arm, the smaller the amount of force, but the action is more immediate.

To exert great force, one must have a force arm as long as possible.

This is a common experience for anyone who has moved rocks with a crowbar—to move heavy rocks with a constant muscular force, use a long crowbar. Similarly, in holding the arm of an opponent to the ground the greatest moment of force and greatest mechanical advantage exists when the arm is grasped as near to the hand as possible, and with the arm extended at right angles to the body, to create a maximally long force arm. Quick turns of the opponent can be produced by using a shorter force arm. Successful grappling relies upon achieving leverage advantages against an opponent: Wing Chun techniques assume from the start that you will have no strength advantage over an opponent.

The concept of balance or stability is equally as important to grappling and throwing as the concept of leverage. The following points relate to the degree of stability of a body:

1. Stability is directly proportional to the area of the base upon which the body rests. It follows therefore that in kicking, one is relatively unstable when one foot is off the ground. This is the reason why Wing Chun is so preoccupied with the idea of the "root of the tree" and generally does not perform high kicks in combat.

2. Stability is indirectly proportional to the distance of the center of gravity of the body above the base. The center of gravity of a body is a point from which the body can be suspended in perfect balance. It is located roughly at the height of the hips on the human body but changes position with a change in position of parts of the body. It is possible, for example, to prevent oneself from being thrown by lowering the center of gravity by sinking into a deep horse-stance. On the other hand, to move fast, keep the center of gravity high.

3. For stability to exist, the center of gravity of a body must fall within its base. Therefore, to throw someone, the body must be moved from its vertical position above the base or stance, to a position where the center of gravity falls outside the base or stance.

4. Stability is directly proportional to the weight of the body: the heavier man is harder to throw than the lighter man.

These principles of balance are of great use in all types of throwing activities. Nevertheless, they do not fully or adequately describe the type of throwing employed in Wing Chun, whose throwing involves getting the body to follow a point of pain—for example, in the case of a rear choke, hold the neck in such a way that you force the opponent to throw himself to avoid the pain of the lock. Serious injury results from holding the body part causing the pain while the opponent falls. I shall now describe in more detail this style of fighting, and further caution the reader not to use these techniques in sparring: they are designed especially for the street.

WING CHUN'S GRABBING AND DISABLING THROWS

I shall now give a concise summary of the principle types of disabling throws in Wing Chun. As I have said before, these throwing techniques are economical, simple, and totally oriented toward street fighting self-defense.

Arm-bar throws. This family of throws is concerned with pressure applied against the elbow, involving straightening the elbow and applying pressure against the elbow joint. There are a variety of ways of using the arm-bar to put an opponent on the ground, disabled. For example, against a straight punch, you defend with a *til sao,* grabbing the arm at the wrist. Your other hand locks up the upper portion of the opponent's arm with a dropping palm (or *fook sao*), which is turned so that the fingers point toward the ground. The opponent's leg is simultaneously kicked away with the *til toi* kick from the sticky-leg techniques. Holding the arm while the opponent falls, or jerking in the opposite direction to the fall can severely damage both the elbow and the shoulder.

Another use of the arm-bar technique occurs in sticky-hand fighting. You perform a grab-and-chop technique on an opponent, pulling his arm down and aiming a chop at his throat. He defends against the chop with a *taun sao.* You cut down this *taun sao* and cross his arms, trapping them. The bottom arm can be used now as a lever against the top arm. Stepping into his body, you may throw him using your hip or leg as an axis of rotation, or simply break his arm at the elbow then and there.

Wrist attacks. There are five basic ways of applying wrist locks: 1) the flex, forcing the palm toward the inner part of the forearm; 2) bending the back of the hand toward the top side of the forearm; 3) the outside twist, turning the hand counterclockwise; 4) the inside twist, turning the hand clockwise; and 5) lateral twisting, twisting the edge of the hand toward the forearm, or the thumb-side of the hand toward the forearm. When a wrist-lock or arm-bar is secured, take a quick step backwards, so that your opponent is swung in a circle. This generates angular momentum that enables you to plough him into the ground, or perhaps into a wall. Throwing is not just a matter of putting someone on the ground, it is a matter of more generally destroying balance.

The chicken-wing bong sao. The chicken-wing *bong sao* was discussed in the *Chum Kil* section. The principal use of this hand is to break the elbow or dislocate the shoulder—the *bong sao* is placed close to the elbow to break the elbow and close to the shoulder to dislocate the shoulder. The idea here is that in close fighting, if you can grab the opponent's wrist and jerk his arm across your chest, your other arm can be swung against either the elbow or upper arm. If your legs are in front of his, the forward throw generated by the swing of his body is likely to break or dislocate the arm. If your legs are behind the opponent it is unlikely that you will severely damage his arm.

Neck lock. From a neck lock using the *Bil Jee* circling footwork, walk one foot behind the opponent. You may then throw the opponent over your hip, or throw him using a leg technique (to be described in volume three) from section seven of the wooden-dummy. A potentially fatal throw can be performed by holding onto the opponent's neck as his body falls.

A moral to be drawn from this is that if you are caught in a head lock, don't try and break the lock by trying to unbalance, sweep, or throw your opponent. If he holds onto your neck, you risk a fatal neck injury. Against any neck attack, always concentrate upon breaking the lock, even if it means breaking your opponent's fingers.

Two simple throws. In conclusion, I shall list two simple throws that anyone can do with a minimum of effort, but which are quite effective. In the first throw, move into the opponent on the side, locking up his leg using *chi gerk*. Force him over your leg by dropping an elbow on his solar plexus (*see* Figure 68). The natural tendency of the body after receiving a sharp blow on the solar plexus is for it to spring back: some young Wing Chun students often try to impress the uninformed public with the power of their one-inch punch by striking a person on the solar plexus (ask them to do a one-inch punch on someone's shoulder!). The result of the strike is that the opponent topples backward over your leg which acts as a fulcrum.

Another useful type of throw that is good for preventing counterattacks is to literally use the opponent's own body to cut off his attack and then force him to throw himself. The idea here is to initiate an attack, such as a grab-and-punch and simultaneous knee kick. Step down with the leg, the left leg to lock up the right leg, or vice versa. The opponent defends against the punch. Now pull your opponent down at a 45-degree angle, so that he virtually falls over himself. The fight will then be in your corner.

48   49   50

GRAPPLING AND THROWING
TECHNIQUES (*CHIN-NA*)

48. The larger fighter delivers a punch that is deflected by the smaller fighter's *til sao* or upper-deflective wrist-movement.

49. Then the smaller fighter jerks the larger forward, pulling him onto a powerful heel-kick to the lower ribs.

50. The smaller fighter then steps down onto the larger fighter's knee and begins to apply a modified hammer-lock.

51. Here you can see the completed modified hammer-lock. The conventional hammer-lock involves twisting an opponent's arm upward behind his back. The modified hammer-lock incorporates the conventional hammer-lock, a wrist lock, and a nerve-center attack, using a claw-hand on the trapezius muscle.

52. From the situation depicted in Figure 48, the smaller fighter may counter-attack by using the arm-bar. This position has been reached by stepping in from the back foot. The smaller fighter can fling the opponent into a wall by stepping backward with his left foot; this generates momentum and gets the opponent off balance, flinging him in a circle, while the smaller fighter pulls the opponent's arm in the opposite direction.

53. Alternatively, another *chin-na* move can be employed from the basic arm-bar. This involves using the chicken wing, or low *bong sao* (described in volume one) to apply pressure to the shoulder joint.

54. Here, you can see the results of using the chicken wing *bong sao* to wrench at the shoulder joint. This technique can be used to attack

51   52   53

54   55   56

either the shoulder or the elbow and is especially effective in the form of a disabling throw where the opponent's body weight is used to hurt his own joints. As has been described already, this is done by stepping backward and flinging the opponent in a circle, while putting pressure on his elbow joint.

55. Another type of throw employing a simple arm-bar is shown here. This time, the *par toi* kick/sweep is used to sweep the larger fighter's leg, so that he falls over sideways.

56. Wrist locks can also be used in throwing. Here, the larger fighter has bent over to escape the pain of a wrist lock. He is about to be pile-driven face-first into the ground, as the smaller fighter shifts his body weight forward, by falling down on him.

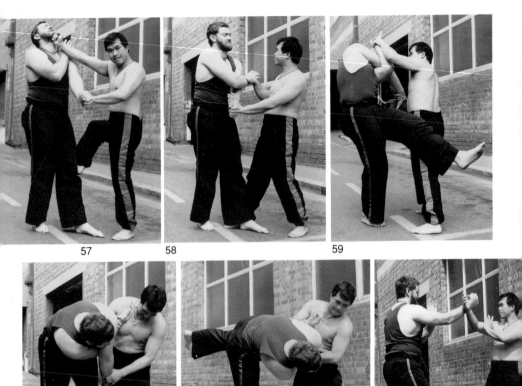

57   58   59

60   61   62

57. From the situation depicted in Figure 48, a simultaneous grab-and-punch and knee kick is delivered.

58. The smaller Wing Chun fighter then steps down and traps the arms as we have seen demonstrated previously.

59. Now a twisting arm-bar is applied, pulling the arms as if turning a wheel. The larger fighter's foot is lifted using the circling-leg-sweep from the *Bil Jee* and he is thrown sideways.

60. The same technique can also be applied when twisting in the opposite direction.

61. This time, the opponent is thrown forward, rather than backward, especially when the supporting foot is swept.

62. Consider now another combat situation. A straight punch is

63

64

65

66

67

thrown by the larger fighter, but the smaller fighter deflects it with a *til sao*.

63. The smaller fighter moves forward, applying an elbow crank.

64. As the larger fighter is pulled backward, in agony from the attack on his elbow, his foot is swept and the larger fighter crashes to the ground, having fallen backward.

65. A similar type of throw is shown here, this time involving a crushing claw-hand to the trachea.

66. Here is a typical sticky-hand combat situation: the smaller fighter's grab-and-chop has been defended by a *taun sao*.

67. The smaller fighter slams his elbow into his opponent's chest as powerfully as possible, stunning him by this unexpected move. The larger fighter's *taun sao* loses some force.

68

69

70

68. An arm-bar is then performed and the smaller fighter uses his own body as a fulcrum. The larger fighter's leg is lifted by using a skill that was described in the sticky-leg section and delivering an explosive elbow smash to the solar plexus. The larger fighter topples over backward.

69. A variation of this skill employs a forearm smash to the throat.

70. As before, the foot is swept and a second elbow-strike delivered. Wing Chun throwing techniques are always part of a striking sequence and are employed strictly for self-defense to disable an opponent.

> Note: All throws in Wing Chun are disabling throws designed to break limbs, not merely to put an opponent on the ground. They are therefore purely self-defense techniques, and unlike the throws of judo, can have no sports application at all.

Dar Mak: Vital Strikes to the Weak Points of Human Anatomy

INTRODUCTION

In this chapter I shall outline the theory of *dar mak,* or vital strikes to weak points of the body. This subject has mistakenly been referred to as *dim mak,* or the theory of the poison or death touch, which implies that someone may be killed or injured by a touch. According to some sources, some martial-arts experts can kill a person by action at a distance—without even touching them! Here I am not concerned with such occult matters, although I wonder why people don't drop dead everyday from accidental death-touches? The theory of *dar mak,* in my opinion, is that one must strike—not merely touch—a set of vital acupuncture points that are coordinated with certain secret times of the day and the seasons of the year. The degree of vulnerability of such vital pressure points depends on these times. The theory of *dar mak* involves striking these points at a certain time so as to damage the circulation of *chi* in the body.

ACUPUNCTURE AND *DAR MAK*

There are some 365 major acupuncture points on the body; since they are usually bilateral with respect to the median axis of the body, there are more than 700 points. These points are linked by 14 major meridians, which serve to direct the flow of *chi* within the body.

Twelve of these meridians are related to the internal organs of the body. (Note that when Chinese medicine refers to an organ, it indicates not just the physical organ itself but the entirety of its functions. Note also that Chinese medicine includes two organs unknown to Western science: the heart constrictor and the triple heater.) These major organs each have their own corresponding meridian (regular meridian), and these are also connected to each other. These organs are in turn classified as being either yin or yang, and two organs in a pair may influence one another. The mother-child law of acupuncture states, for example, that the preceding organ in an energy cycle is the mother, the following organ, is the son, and that by treating the mother, yin or yang can be increased or decreased in an organ to restore health. The noon-midnight law of acupuncture states that organs have a particular time of the day and a season of the year which is best for treatment. This law, as we have already seen, is central to the theory of *dar mak.*

It is not possible to discuss such a complicated subject as acupuncture in any further detail here. I will simply summarize some of the most important *dar mak* points, omitting mention of times and seasons for the strikes. Typically, the person being attacked who needs to perform such strikes has no time to consult a watch before defending himself; and, for that matter, the whole idea of the vulnerability of the body at some specific time is for the Western mind, scientifically suspect. Indeed, for physiological reasons most *dar mak* points are serious strike points at any time. To further substantiate this point, I shall also summarize material relating to the modern medical theory of vital strikes. Taken together, this material is enough for the student of Wing Chun to apply in practical self-defense situations that are also life-threatening. I by no means advocate the use of such violence, outside of self-defense situations.

Before presenting my summary, however, it is necessary to explain how the theory of *dar mak* relates to Wing Chun kung-fu. *Dar mak* may be mistakenly called *dim mak* because the typical strike involves hitting the opponent's body with a striking surface of the body that has a small surface area, typically used for touching, such as the fingers. However, the resultant strike produces an enormous pressure on impact and can damage the body. Such surfaces include the phoenix-eye fist (the sharp second knuckle of the index finger) or the fingertips. In Wing Chun, an entire form, the *Bil Jee* form, is devoted to fingertip strikes, so *dar mak* strikes are typically made with the fingertips. The student who wishes to train in this form of fighting is advised to strengthen and condition the fingers in the ways previously described in chapter four of volume one in this series.

Knowledge of the weaknesses of human anatomy is not necessarily only of use for developing one's offensive weapons. Such knowledge can make martial-arts training, especially full-contact sparring, safer, as students realize the possibility of certain blows being fatal. Therefore, the study of the weaknesses of human anatomy in a martial-arts context is not an immoral activity. It is the abuse of such knowledge that is ethically problematic.

There is no space here to discuss the issue of brain damage in full-contact martial arts. I recommend that the reader consult: A. Guterman and R. Smith, "Neurological Sequelae of Boxing," *Sports Medicine* 4 (1987): 194–210.

SUMMARY OF THE MOST IMPORTANT *DAR MAK* POINTS IN TRADITIONAL CHINESE MEDICINE

1. *Pai hui* point — located in the middle of the upper head. Fatal point.
2. *Chi men* point — (Adam's apple) heavy strikes may result in suffocation.
3. *Tang men* point — located in the middle of the chest slightly below the nipples. Fatal point.
4. *Shen chueh* point — located on the navel. Heavy strikes result in internal bleeding.
5. *Hui yin* point — located on the peritoneum. Heavy strikes are thought by the Chinese to result in loss of life. (questionable)
6. *Nao hu* point — under the occipital at the back of the head. Fatal point.
7. *Tien hsi* point — at rear of ear. Fatal point.
8. *Pei liang* point — on the seventh cervical vertebra. Fatal point.
9. *Ming men* point — on the second lumbar vertebra. Fatal point.
10. Temple point — fatal point.

11. *Chiang tai* point — two inches above the breast nipples. Heart and lung damage with possible death.
12. *Yung chuan* point — in the middle of the sole of the foot. Thought not only to paralyze the foot but also to damage the brain.
13. *Chien ching* point—located in the front of the shoulder. Paralyzes arm.
14. *Yao men* point — on the spinal cord in the location of the vocal cord of the neck. Speechlessness if struck.
15. *Feng wei* point — between the seventh and eighth vertebrae diagonally under the arm pit in the location of the rear of the lung. Lung damage.
16. *Ching chu* point — left is the spleen position, right is the liver location. Paralysis point.
17. *Hsiao yao* point — kidney position. Paralysis point.
18. *Wun mei* point — middle of the wrist. Paralysis of hand.
19. *Tai chung* point — gap between bones of first and second toes on foot. Numbs foot.
20. *Tsi ku* point—middle of the elbow joint, soft flesh area. Paralysis of arm.
21. *Tien chu* point—sides of the neck across from the *yao men* point. Paralysis point.
22. *Pi yu* point—inner side of the middle of the upper arm. Paralysis of arm.
23. *Tsi chu* point — middle of the elbow joint. Paralysis of the arm.
24. Tiger's mouth point—gap between thumb and forefinger. Paralysis of hand.
25. *Pai high* point — on the upper thigh, four inches below lower abdomen. Paralysis of leg.
26. *Wei chun* point — back of the knee joint. Paralysis of leg, knee damage.
27. *Chu ping* point — back of the leg in the middle of the widest part of the calf muscle. Paralysis of lower leg.
28. *Dan tien* point — one inch below navel. Considered to be one of the most important *chi kung* points of the body. Strikes thought to damage heart, lungs, and brain.
29. *Kuan yuan* point—three inches below the navel. Kidney damage.

EXAMPLES OF FATAL TIMES FOR *DAR MAK* IN TRADITIONAL CHINESE MEDICINE
(controversial and problematic)

1. Kidney: kills at 11 P.M.
2. Tail bone: kills at 12 P.M.
3. The clavicle, hit in a downward position: kills at 4 A.M.
4. Two inches below the nipples: kills between 7–8 A.M.
5. Stomach: kills at 3 P.M.
6. Liver: kills at 9 A.M.
7. Penis: kills at 11 A.M.

SUMMARY OF THE MODERN MEDICAL THEORY OF VITAL STRIKES

1. *Top of head (coronal suture):* this is the join of the two frontal and parietal bones of the cranium, and is a weak point in the skull. A powerful blow may result in a skull fracture, hemorrhage, and death.

2. *Forehead:* light to severe concussion. A concussion is a shaking of the brain within the brain case. Severe rupturing of the vessels in the membrane surrounding the brain may result in a brain hemorrhage with resultant death. Furthermore, the trigeminal nerve lies just below the center point of the forehead, and if struck may produce impaired vision and temporary or permanent paralysis.

3. *Ears:* concussion again; rupture of the eardrum and damage to the inner ear will affect balance, rendering an opponent helpless. The mastoids, located just behind the ear, may be attacked by gouging fingertip pressure to produce incredible pain.

4. *Temple:* fracture in the temporal region of the skull; pinching or severing of the meningeal artery resulting in a brain hemorrhage and death.

5. *Glabella:* directly between the eyebrows. A blow here directly damages the frontal lobes of the brain, resulting in concussion, unconsciousness, and death.

6. *Eyes:* rupture of the eyeball; pain with possible permanent blindness. A powerful *bil jee* could destroy the eyes, penetrate the brain, and result in death.

7. *Bridge of nose:* fracture; dislocation of the nasal bone and

septum, massive bleeding. Not usually death dealing in itself, but if unconsciousness occurs, death may result from concussion when the head hits the ground.

8. *Under the nose:* a powerful blow produces at best a bursting fracture of the skull; also extensive bleeding may occur from damage to the front teeth and gums. The Chinese believe that a sharp blow here will render one unconscious.

9. *The nose, from below:* death may result by a 45-degree upward palm-strike forcing the septal cartilage through the crista galli into the brain like a spear. (controversial)

10. *Jaw:* fracture of the jaw, unconsciousness, and concussion if struck from below on the tip of the jaw. Powerful strikes may result in severe shock to the cerebellum and cerebral hemispheres, leading to death. A whiplash injury to the neck may also occur. Horizontal strikes to the jaw may result in fractures to the lower jaw and cheekbones. The facial nerve may also be pinched, resulting in paralysis of the face.

11. *Throat:* rupturing of the internal jugular vein, resulting in death by hemorrhage. Contusion of the carotid vein may result in blood clotting in the vessels of the brain with the possibility of death. Damage to the vagus nerve on either side of the neck, which controls heart contraction and lung constriction, may result in fatal heart palpitations and breathing difficulties. Injury to the phrenic nerve, which controls the actions of the diaphragm, may also lead to death, through the inability to breathe. Other targets on the throat include the esophagus, Adam's Apple, and trachea (wind pipe). An attack on the trachea may result in death by asphyxiation and blood drowning. In general throat attacks involve: 1) cutting off the blood supply to the brain; 2) cutting off air by choking; 3) the damage listed above by direct strikes; and 4) breaking the neck by any number of neck locks and cranks (e.g., front neck-lift, front face-lift, etc.).

12. *Back of neck:* minimum damage is a whiplash injury to the neck. If the spinal cord is severed lower than the fifth cervical vertebra, complete paralysis results from the point of the break downward. Severing above the fifth cervical vertebra will be fatal.

13. *Collar bone:* severance or laceration damage to the bronchial nerve will cause paralysis of the arm. A powerful blow may push the

broken bone into the lung, collapsing it. Air starvation, uncontrollable spasms of the heart, coma, and death will follow.

14. *Sternum:* effects range from the production of intense pain to cardio-respiratory damage.

15. *Xiphoid process:* this is a cartilaginous attachment to the sternum. As the heart lies almost directly against the sternum, a penetrating strike to the xiphoid on a rising 45-degree plane may break it off and force it through the heart.

16. *Solar plexus:* striking this nerve center may cause contraction of the diaphragm, instantly winding an opponent; sometimes accompanied by unconsciousness.

17. *Heart:* the heart can be attacked by snapping concussive blows left of the center-line of the chest.

18. *Side of rib cage:* powerful kicks and punches may result in broken ribs, puncturing, and collapsing the lung.

19. *Floating ribs:* the eleventh and twelfth ribs are not connected to the sternum by costal cartilage. These ribs can be broken relatively easily, damaging the liver or stomach.

20. *Lungs:* the lungs may be damaged by a powerful blow to a target area of about one inch below the nipple on the left and right sides. A blow at this point exerts maximum leverage against the ribs.

21. *Spleen:* splinters of rib bones may pierce the spleen, resulting in internal hemorrhaging with unconsciousness, coma, and death.

22. *Kidney:* kidney strikes may result in bursting of the kidney, producing excruciating pain. Without artificial support, destruction of both the left and right kidney will lead to certain death from uremia (the presence of toxic urinary material in the blood). The kidneys are prone to massive hemorrhage when struck strongly, and the shock from a kidney injury can be very severe.

23. *Bladder:* rupture of the full bladder may lead to death through uremia.

24. *Diaphragm:* unconsciousness due to respiratory paralysis and brain damage due to oxygen starvation may occur, and if normal breathing does not resume within minutes, death will result.

25. *Biceps muscle:* strong chops to the musculocutane nerve and the median nerve can paralyze the arm, making blocking impossible.

26. *Triceps muscle:* as above; strikes can result in paralysis of the arm, making punching impossible.

27. *Elbow:* a blow slightly above the elbow joint may result in a fracture of the humerus. Injury to the bronchial artery may lead to gangrene which may require amputation.

28. *Coccyx:* a powerful blow here will produce paralysis. It is best attacked by a knee strike from behind, jerking the opponent's body back onto the strike. Damage to this area is particularly inconvenient, as the anal muscles are attached to the coccyx, so that bowel movements will involve pulling against the broken or fractured coccyx.

29. *Groin:* rupture of the bladder, fracture of the pubic bone, nausea, vomiting, and unconsciousness may occur.

30. *Underside of thigh:* muscle spasm, fractured or dislocated femur; herniation of the muscle tissues.

31. *Back of knee:* thrusting the knee forward and the upper body back may tear all of the muscles of the knee; dislocation of the knee joint; shock, nausea, and severe pain will occur.

32. *Front of knee:* heavy blows may tear the semi-lunar cartilage or produce an avulsion fracture with torn ligaments.

33. *Achilles tendon:* ranges from a sprained ankle or numbing of the foot, to fractures of the bone of the foot and ankle. Destruction of the tendon itself will mean the inability to move the foot, leaving the opponent's offense and defense considerably weakened.

REFERENCES

B.C. Adams, *Medical Implications of Karate Blows* (New York: A.S. Barnes and Co., 1969).

Hei Long, *Dragon's Touch: Weaknesses of the Human Anatomy* (Colorado: Paladin Press, 1983).

D.H.Y. Hsieh, *Advanced Dim Mak* (Hawaii: McLisa Enterprises, 1983).

J.S.H. Lin, *Poison Hand Touch of Death* (Hawaii: McLisa Enterprises, 1982).

N. Mashiro, *Black Medicine: The Dark Art of Death* (Colorado: Paladin Press, 1978).

B.J. Steiner, *The Death Dealer's Manual* (Colorado: Paladin Press, 1982).

5

Toward an Enrichment of the Wing Chun System

THE LIMITS OF WING CHUN KUEN

The strengths of a system are also its weaknesses. Many masters of the martial arts are unwilling to acknowledge any limitations to their style. Other masters acknowledge certain limits, but seem unconcerned about improving their styles by overcoming these limits, because it will mean breaking with tradition. Accepting a technique as being good merely because it has been practiced for decades or even centuries, is not in my opinion a good and rational reason for practicing it, if the aim of the martial arts is effective combat rather than cultural or spiritual studies. A good technique, in my opinion, is one that has a solid scientific, biomechanical foundation, and that, along with appropriate strategies, works in combat. A good martial-art system must also be judged by the same criteria of having a coherent system of techniques, each with a rational biomechanical basis, linked together with sound logistics.

If we look at Wing Chun kung-fu from a rational, scientific, and logistic perspective, we can see that many of Wing Chun's strengths are also its weaknesses. These weaknesses relate to both hand and leg techniques. Wing Chun is a small-circle system: its hand and leg techniques are especially designed for close-range combat. It is true of course that the *Bil Jee* form has many long fist techniques, but this form does not constitute in itself a complete long-range fighting art. On the subject of hand-striking techniques, Wing Chun relies in general upon straight-line attacks, because the shortest distance between two points is a straight line. However, sometimes it would be strategically advantageous to use circular attacks to loop under, over, or around an opponent's straight-line attacks to deliver the knockout power of a long fist style. The Wing Chun punch is not known as a one-punch to kill—damage is done by the cumulative effect of multiple punches. The art would be improved if the more powerful punching techniques could be added without compromising the style.

The same two points can also be made about Wing Chun's kicking. In combat, Wing Chun relies upon low kicks, especially in sticky-leg (*chi gerk*) fighting. Circular kicks, such as the roundhouse kick, do not occur in the traditional system of Wing Chun. Nor for that matter do other kicks that have proved to be effective in kickboxing, such as the snap-kick, axe-kick, or side-kick. Now the side-footage kick in the *Chum Kil* form is a kick in which the foot does not travel in a straight line; rather, the foot moves in an arc. If the received system can include such a non-Wing Chun kick, then why not add others, providing the use of these kicks is consistent with the basic Wing Chun philosophy? I see no such reason.

The limitations of Wing Chun can, I believe, be overcome by adding to the system the hand skills of White Crane kung-fu (*Pak Hok Kuen*) and the kicking, knee, and elbow work of Thai boxing (*Muay Thai*). This new system or style shall be called *Sun Tzu Kuen*. The style is named after the great Chinese military thinker Sun Tzu (*see* Sun Tzu, *The Art of War*, trans. S.B. Griffith [Oxford: Clarendon Press, 1964]). *Sun Tzu Kuen* is not just Wing Chun, White Crane, and Thai Boxing techniques randomly mixed together, but is a genuine reconciliation and unification of three styles that on the surface seem to be based on contradictory philosophies of combat. As I argue in this chapter, it is possible to systematically reconcile three different styles to produce a complete fighting system.

WHITE CRANE KUNG-FU (*PAK HOK KUEN*)

According to legend, the originator of *Pak Hok Kuen*, or White Crane kung-fu, was the monk Adato (b. A.D. 1426) who lived at the beginning of Hsuan Tsung's reign in the Ming Dynasty. Adato was ordained a monk in Tibet. There he had learned Chinese wrestling or *chin-na,* but was not content with the martial-art skills that he possessed. He retreated to the mountains to live a secluded life, so that he could meditate, study the Buddhist canons, and practice martial arts without interruption. It was there that he witnessed a fight between a crane and an ape. The crane, with its evasive footwork and quick attacks, was more than a match for the powerful, aggressive attacks of the ape. Inspired by this battle, Adato went on to develop his own style of martial arts based upon techniques of both the ape and the crane, calling his style "Lion's Roar." Adato's style consisted of eight fists, eight stances, eight finger attacks, eight palm techniques, eight seizing techniques, and eight kicking techniques: the so-called octave theory. These basic hand and foot techniques were then organized into three forms: the Flying Crane form, the *Nilad* form, and the *Dolo* form.

The monk Logutwun changed the title of Adato's style to *Pak Hok,* meaning White Crane, because the name Lion's Roar was a somewhat arrogant assertion of martial-art supremacy that could only invite trouble. Logutwun worked to improve and simplify the system. This process of simplification and improvement was continued during the Ching Dynasty by the monk Hsing Lung and his disciples, who took the art to South China in the Chao Ching district of Kuangtung (Canton). There it spread throughout Kuangtung and eventually to the West.

The White Crane system today consists of fourteen basic hand and ten weapon sets, including *Luk Lek Kuen* (boxing form of six forces), *Chuit Yap Bo* (advance and retreat stances), and the needle wrapped in cotton set. This last set is a form of internal *kung* where emphasis is placed upon breathing (*chi kung*), and the unity of the mind and body. Associated with this form is a set of teachings relating to strikes to the weak points of the human anatomy. Here I am concerned only with the basic hand moves of the White Crane system: these moves in themselves constitute in essence a powerful system of fighting. It is my aim to add these long fist techniques to the Wing Chun system.

The philosophy of White Crane kung-fu was originally fully

expressed by Adato by four Chinese characters: *chan* (ruthlessness), *shan* (evasiveness), *chuan* (penetration), and *tsieh* (interception). These points can be summarized as follows:

1. *Chan:* the very point of White Crane kung-fu is to fight, to be able to defend oneself. While some Chinese and Japanese styles are concerned with the spiritual qualities of a martial art, the White Crane fighter is concerned with how to survive combat—potential life-and-death situations. The offensive hand techniques of this system are extremely powerful, especially designed for killing with one strike. In South China's White Crane system, an emphasis is put upon this aspect of the ape's fighting skill; in the West, there is a tendency to be concerned with the softer aspects of the art, based upon the graceful movements of the crane.

2. *Shan:* this means to evade. In the South China form of White Crane kung-fu, there are very few defensive hand moves: it is believed that blocking or even soft-style deflections are too time consuming. The fighter prefers to use footwork to walk away from attacks and then counterattack. Hard force can be used to counter an opponent's attack provided the softest and weakest part of the attacking weapon is struck. I shall discuss this point in more detail later.

3. *Chuan:* this means to penetrate. The White Crane fighter, because of, as we shall soon see, the unusual stance adopted in fighting, is very concerned with timing. Attacks must be made when the opponent least expects them and can least deal with them. The White Crane fighter is preoccupied with setting up an opponent and defeating him quickly and efficiently.

4. *Tsieh:* this means to intercept. Attacks may be intercepted in either a soft or a hard fashion. Soft interception involves using evasive footwork or flexible body turning to allow blows to pass by harmlessly. In hard interception, an opponent's attack is countered as soon as it is initiated, frequently by attacking the weak points of the opponent's arms or legs. The philosophy here is to destroy the serpent by destroying his fangs, a point of view also accepted by Wing Chun fighters.

The White Crane fighting stance is unusual. The fighter faces an opponent side-on with the lead hand fully extended, fingers up, and palm facing the opponent as if to signal to him: stop and come no further. The lead hand is held at roughly shoulder height. It is never held in a stiff and inflexible fashion; rather, it is constantly fluttering in the air, keeping the opponent's attention. The other arm is held behind your back such that the opponent cannot see it. This unseen arm is the principal striking arm, with attacks coming from a wide range of possible angles.

When first confronted with this aspect of the White Crane system, many martial artists believe that no one could possibly fight effectively in this fashion, that the stance from the waist up is hopelessly open. Do not be fooled: a skillful White Crane fighter is no push-over. First, he is in constant and meaningful motion, searching for your opening and angle of weakness. Second, you do not know where the attack is coming from: will it be from overhead; from below; from some side angle; or will it be a straight punch? Third, the White Crane fighter uses his attacks to cover himself. As I have said, in the South China form of White Crane kung-fu, there are few hand blocks and deflections. Defense and offense are collapsed into one: an attack should, with the appropriate footwork, be an adequate defense. The circular long-armed attacks should cover the body.

The other unusual feature of South China's White Crane kung-fu is its use of the wide horse-stance in fighting. Western White Crane fighters tend to regard the primary function of the wide horse-stance as an exercise to strengthen the legs. For the Chinese White Crane fighter, the wide horse-stance and walking stance are used to give a solid foundation for executing techniques. This is not to say that other stances are not used; indeed, the White Crane fighter may use a variety of stances such as the normal walking stance used in daily life. Kicking attacks, for example, are usually executed from the shoulder-width stance (normal standing position). However, the execution of attacks requires a solid foundation that cannot be adequately supplied by any high stances. Just as a powerful cannon requires a wide base to maintain its balance while firing, so does the White Crane fighter adopt a wide stance to maintain his balance while firing full-power long arm attacks.

In the South China form of White Crane kung-fu, there is such a great emphasis placed upon balance and stability that kicking is not favored as a means of attack. If kicking is attempted, it is usually used with a simultaneous hand attack, or to set up an opponent for a hand attack. By contrast, Western White Crane styles, with their higher stances, have many excellent kicking skills, usually specializing in double kicks such as the double jumping roundhouse kick, double axe-kick, double snap-kick, and so on. Wing Chun kung-fu has much in common in combat philosophy with Southern China's White Crane kung-fu.

There are seven basic hand attacks. As I have said, the system is not concerned with blocking and deflecting, so great skill and power must be achieved with these hand moves if successful fighting is to be accomplished. The basic hand moves are as follows:

1. *Chin:* the White Crane straight punch, is a powerful punch executed with body rotation to add momentum to the punch. The basic strategy used with this punch is to counterattack either over or under an opponent's attack. As in karate, impact is made on the two largest knuckles of the fist.

2. *Pow:* the White Crane throwing punch or long upper cut, represents another angle of attack that can be made by use of the hidden back hand. Unlike the upper cut seen in Western boxing, the striking surface in the White Crane punch is with the sharp second knuckles of the fist, to maximize the pressure of impact. This attack is usually made against soft areas of the body such as the testicles, kidneys, or throat.

3. *Kup:* the White Crane overhead strike complements the *pow* strike. Impact is made with the sharp knuckles of the fist against the temple, nose, or top of the head. *Kup* is also used against kicks: the strategy here is to paralyze the opponent's leg by striking the soft muscles of the leg (such as the back of the knee or the calf muscle) and then move in for the kill. This vicious way of dealing with kicking attacks makes the White Crane style unsuitable for tournament fighting. Indeed, even against hand attacks, the White Crane fighter attacks the forearm muscles, biceps, and triceps until a guard drops and a destructive punch can be delivered.

4. *Dang:* the double downward back-fist, illustrates another interesting point about the White Crane system: that it is especially designed for fighting more than one person. *Dang* is used to attack two opponents from high to low. Target areas include the top of the head, face, side of head, and shoulder muscles.

5. *Bin:* the double horizontal back-fist, is also used to simultaneously attack two foes. In executing both *dang* and *bin,* the arms are first drawn in to the body, and then flung out either downward in the case of *dang* or horizontally in the case of *bin.*

6. *Jow:* the clawing hand of the White Crane system, is used primarily to tear and rip rather than to lock and grapple. The clawing technique, in contrast to the other hand moves, is executed by using the front hand.

7. *Chow:* the horizontal hooking punch, does not differ substantially in its use from the hook in boxing. It is also worth noting that a punch midway between the *Pow* and *Kup* can also be used as a hook punch, capable of hooking around guards and contacting with the sharp knuckles on weak points of human anatomy.

UNIFYING AND RECONCILING WING CHUN AND WHITE CRANE KUNG-FU

The main difficulty in reconciling Wing Chun and White Crane kung-fu is not footwork. The wide horse-stance is not unknown in Wing Chun and is used in the six-and-a-half pole techniques, and sometimes for stability and power in butterfly-knife fighting in thrusting the knives. Of course, you cannot effectively kick from this stance, but neither do White Crane fighters, preferring a shoulder-width stance for kicking. Incidentally, the fact that a shoulder-width free sparring stance is used by White Crane fighters for kicking is one fact that enables the link up between the divergent styles of White Crane Kung-fu and *Muay Thai.* However, to return to the main discussion, I see the main difficulty in using White Crane hand techniques at a long fist range and Wing Chun skills at a closer range, lying in the apparent openness of the White Crane stance. Doesn't this violate the center-line theory of Wing Chun?

If we look closely at the White Crane system, we find that it, too, uses a center-line theory. The center-line runs down the side of the body instead of the front of the body. Overhead and underarm attacks are still made through a plane containing the center-line, and in fact these attacks are the White Crane fighter's way of defending his center-line. It is also a mistake to suppose that at a distance the White Crane fighter is wide open. His body is defended by the deceptive behind-the-back strike as well as excellent footwork. At a closer distance, the White Crane stance may be open to classical Wing Chun attacks, but the *Sun Tzu Kuen* fighter then fights using Wing Chun techniques or he may use close-range *Muay Thai* techniques. I therefore feel that there is no technical problem about using the White Crane system to fight at a long fist distance and then changing to a Wing Chun stance when moving in for in-fighting.

Neither is there any basic irreconcilable philosophical difference between Wing Chun and White Crane kung-fu. First, both styles draw upon the fighting movements of the crane for combat inspiration, and it would be surprising if the two kung-fu styles could be so different as to incorporate mutually irreconcilable techniques. Second, the principles of *chan, shan, chuan,* and *tsieh* are also acceptable to Wing Chun practitioners. All of this suggests that two seemingly different styles have in fact a common combat philosophy as well as complementary elements (White Crane kung-fu lacking the in-fighting merits of Wing Chun) and may be joined together to form a new style, a compound or composite style that consists of two styles, each of which is utilized for a different purpose.

THE FINAL ELEMENT OF *SUN TZU KUEN: MUAY THAI*

The fighting merits of *Muay Thai* cannot be seriously doubted by any kung-fu stylist. This is seen by the simple fact that in 1959, Thai boxers beat Taiwanese kung-fu fighters in five straight fights. The same occurred in 1963 and 1971. The Thai boxers are well known for their superhuman training—not only do they run, skip-rope, do bag work, lift weights, kick bags full of rocks and gravel (and are even rumored to condition their shins with a coke bottle filled with sand), but they gear their training around sparring and ultimately full-contact matches. Techniques that have not proven successful in the ring are abandoned. In addition, the Thais are feared for the viciousness of their fighting techniques. Kicks and punches may be blasted onto an opponent's biceps until the guard drops and the head is open for attack, or the legs are given full-power kicks to destroy the opponent's footwork. In *Muay Thai,* as in Wing Chun, the combat emphasis is upon simplicity and pragmatism.

Modern *Muay Thai* has only one stance, a natural shoulder-width stance, the body weight distributed evenly on both feet. The body is upright, with elbows held in close to the body, the back foot is turned out 45 degrees from the center-line, and the toes of the front foot are turned in slightly. The stance is like a more upright version of the basic walking stance of Wing Chun's *Chum Kil* form. In advancing, *Muay Thai* fighters shuffle the front foot forward, quickly moving the back foot, maintaining the fighting stance while moving. The backward shuffle involves stepping back first with the back foot, then moving the front foot. To move sideways to the right, with the right foot leading, the front foot is moved to the right and slightly advanced, and then the left foot is moved and advanced. To move to the left with the right foot leading, the back foot moves to the left and back and then the front foot is moved left and back. Some fighters regard this footwork as far too slow and advocate springing backward, forward, or sideways as a prawn might do. In either case, this footwork is simple yet highly efficient.

The five basic punches of Western boxing: the lead jab, right (or left) cross, hook, upper cut, and overhand right (or left) are used in *Muay Thai* although the straight jab (*chok*), hook punch (*mat tong*), and upper cut (*mat aat*), are the preferred punches. For knockout power from the arm, the Thais usually rely upon elbow strikes (*sawk*), which are also felt to be safer than punches, as punches leave the body open for knee and round or crocodile-tail kicks (*te*). Many unorthodox styles of Western boxing techniques that work well enough in a boxing ring would get you into a lot of trouble with a Thai boxer. I have in mind any stance with one or both hands down low. The head is liable to be kicked like a football. In addition, the common boxing practice of ducking attacks, dropping the body down and forward, may lead to a knee in the face. Further, as Thai boxing involves grappling (*djab ko*), even though gloves are worn, low hand guards will put one at a disadvantage, making it easier for a devastating technique: an opponent is grabbed around the neck and violently shaken from side to side to destroy his balance, after which his face is smashed by a knee.

The Thai knee and elbow (*sawk*) techniques are also feared techniques. The elbow strike is made in the four possible directions in which the elbow can move—left, right, up, and down, care being taken to put the entire body weight behind each elbow smash. The knee strike is made possible in the three ways in which the knee strike can be made: straight knee rise, roundhouse knee strike, and inside-then-outside knee strike; further, flying knee kicks are sometimes used by lightweight boxers. The *Muay Thai* use of the knee and elbow differs from that in other martial-arts systems in the way in which it is used to virtually cut an opponent to pieces: repeated knee attacks are used to cause immobility, and elbow strikes against the arms are used to destroy the guard. Many Thai fighters have been killed by an elbow smash to the temple.

Thai kicks are not snapping-style kicks that can be retracted if they miss. The philosophy of kicking in *Muay Thai* has always been to commit your body weight to maximize power, so most kicking is done from the back foot, the front foot being used primarily to jab the opponent and feel him out. The Thai round kick differs from the roundhouse kick of other styles in that it involves swinging the leg through the target, exploding body weight through pivoting on the ball of the front foot. The impact is on the well conditioned shin or instep rather than the ball of the foot. The result of this method is a kick that is so powerful that it cannot even be blocked by both forearms. The Thai round kick is an excellent weapon against all high kicking attacks: the cut kick is a special round kick used to attack the supporting leg at the knee when the opponent has his entire body weight on one leg. This produces an extremely bad break of the knee. Front kicks, for example, are not snap kicks, but are push and thrusting kicks used to destroy an opponent's balance and set him up usually for a round kick. I shall say more about this shortly.

Some books and articles on Thai boxing describe Thai defenses as very hard: round kicks are to be taken on the shin or on the forearms. This hard against hard defense is not a preferred defense. Rather, the Thai boxer aims to avoid the attack completely by good footwork, thus preserving energy, and to attack an opponent where he is open. This is a basic principle that all three systems—Wing Chun, White Crane, and *Muay Thai* share. A hard defense is not to be used unless it is necessary against a hard attack (don't absorb punches and kicks) and a hard attack is always to be used against a soft area of the body.

It is worthwhile saying something here about jumping kicks. A vertical jumping kick, where one jumps up into the air vertically and kicks, is weaker than a kick with one foot on the ground. While this style of kick gives you reach, if the body is airborne the kick substantially subjects you to Newton's Third Law of Motion: the reaction at impact will drive your body backward. A football kicked like this will travel only a short distance. If one foot is on the ground then the earth itself provides a reaction due to the force of the nonkicking leg. (*See* R. Groves and D.N. Camaione, *Concepts in Kinesiology* [Philadelphia, W.B. Saunders, 1975], p. 229.) A jumping kick that maximizes power is one in which you jump into your opponent, exploding your entire body weight through him. Therefore when performing jumping kicks, jump or explode into and through your opponent, do not merely jump vertically. This principle is given excellent application in the *Muay Thai* back-foot push kick. The idea here is to explode into your opponent, but instead of snapping the leg, as in a back-foot snap kick, you contact with your opponent's chest and push as if you were doing a leg press. This kick can easily knock an opponent out of the ring, and at a minimum disrupt his balance, setting him up for an attack by round kicks or by the elbow and knees.

The *Sun Tzu Kuen* fighter fights using one of three styles depending upon the combat range and circumstances. At close range, where kicking is impossible, as it would be in a phone booth, sticky-hands, *chin-na,* and clawing techniques are preferred. At medium range, too close for long kicking, but too far to be hit by Wing Chun's running punch, the White Crane long hand techniques are preferred. At a slightly greater distance, *Muay Thai* kicks are available. Of course, there is much overlap, because *Muay Thai* also specializes in in-fighting as well. There is therefore nothing very difficult about using all three styles in practical fighting: simply select the technique to suit the range and circumstances and use that technique effectively to put your opponent down and out. What I have described here constitutes a complete martial-art system incorporating: 1) hand attacks and defenses; 2) leg attacks and defenses; 3) the use of the body (hips, shoulder, as weapons); 4) grappling, clawing, and wrestling; and 5) throwing. It has excellent techniques suitable for all three ranges of combat, because it is a composite style using a different specialized style for each range. Finally, it has merit over some other eclectic styles that may incorporate up to twenty-six different styles.

Excellence in the martial arts is best obtained by mastering simple but effective skills and creatively applying them to whatever challenge faces you; there are no real secret skills in the martial arts, there are only two choices: correct or incorrect methods, and hard or lazy training.

71   72   73

74   75

FROM WING CHUN TO *SUN TZU KUEN:* FIGHTING TECHNIQUES

71. This sequence of photographs illustrates how Thai kick-boxing (*Muay Thai*) techniques may be coherently and effectively added to Wing Chun kung-fu. We begin from the familiar hand-trap position. An elbow smash is delivered to the jaw, stunning the larger fighter.

72. The larger fighter is then grabbed by the hair The smaller fighter takes a step backward and momentarily maintains a wide stance, while preparing for a knee smash.

73. A knee smash is delivered to the chin.

74. The opponent is now pulled violently from side to side with forearm pressure applied to the ears. This will destroy his balance

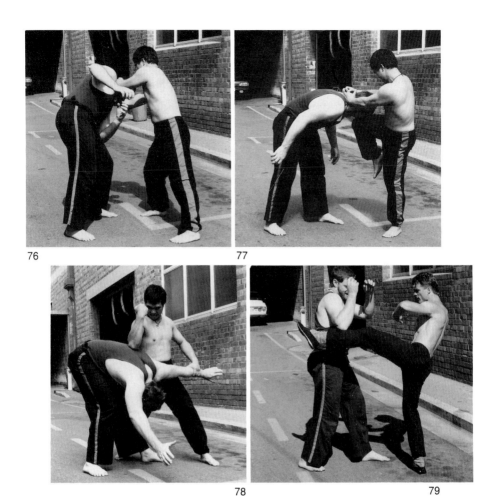

76

77

78

79

and add force to further knee attacks. His ears may be damaged, or severely pained by the forearm pressure, especially if the forearms are slammed or chopped onto the ears in making the neck grab.

75. Another knee smash is delivered.

76. The opponent is now pulled down, ready for another knee smash.

77. A knee smash to the face is delivered.

78. The opponent, having been pulled down by grabbing his left hand, is defeated with an elbow smash to the spine.

79. The following sequence illustrates some sensible ways to defend against kicking attacks. Here the smaller fighter's round-house kick is neutralized by an elbow block. The point of impact is

80   81   82

83   84

the soft calf muscle, not the shin. If you must block (rather than evade), use a hard block against the weakest part of the opponent's leg.

80. Against a front kick, the smaller fighter defends with his knee, attacking his opponent's calf muscle.

81. Against the same attack, the White Crane throwing punch, or *pow,* is equally effective as an attack on the kicking leg

82. In this situation, the larger fighter defends against the smaller fighter's Thai boxing roundhouse kick, by delivering a heel-kick to the groin. Use is made here of the Wing Chun center-line theory. Because a straight kick is faster than a circular kick, all physiological and biomechanical factors being held constant, the fighter can be kicked in the groin before his roundhouse kick can do any damage.

83. The same roundhouse kick may be defended against by retreating and letting it sail past.

85   86

87   88

84. The larger fighter then moves forward, locks up the smaller fighter's arm and leg, and smashes him on the top of the head with a hammer-punch.

85. The smaller fighter now launches a front kick, which the larger fighter side-steps.

86. A rear foot roundhouse kick is now delivered to the head.

87. The smaller fighter has attacked with the popular spinning rear kick. The larger fighter kicks him in the buttocks before the spin is completed. Again, a straight kick is faster than a spinning kick to a fixed target, all other factors held constant. But the spinning kick has tremendous momentum, so it is important to stop the kick early in the spin. If the opponent is very fast, then step back and let the kick go by first before attacking.

88. Here the smaller fighter's front kick is deflected by a *bong sao* and a Wing Chun lifting kick is whipped under the kicking leg into the groin.

89

90

91

92

89. The larger fighter and the smaller fighter square off. The smaller fighter has one hand hidden behind his back in the White Crane fighting stance. It could, and will, be used in a variety of attacks, all unknown and unanticipatable by his opponent.

90. The larger fighter launches a straight punch, which is deflected by the smaller fighter by turning his body; and with the added reach and momentum generated by the turn, he strikes the larger's head with the White Crane *chin*, or straight punch.

91. Then the smaller fighter strikes his opponent's groin with the *pow*, or throwing punch, of the White Crane system.

92. This is followed up with an attack by the White Crane *kup*, or overhead strike, to the bridge of the nose. As the impact is upon the sharp second knuckles, this strike is essentially reserved for attacking the weaker points of human anatomy.

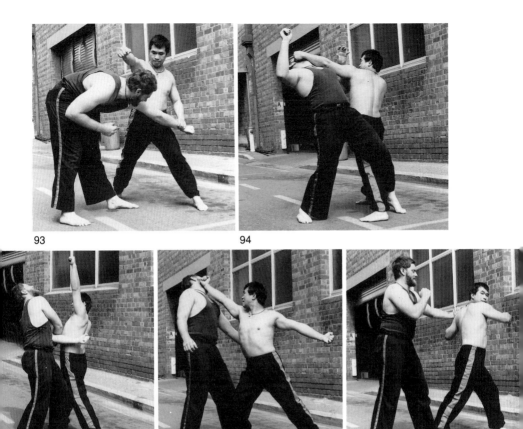

93

94

95

96

97

93. The larger fighter is now pulled down, and another *kup* strike is then delivered to the back of the neck.

94. Another *kup* strike is delivered to the temple.

95. In this sequence we see a typical Wing Chun trap, and the smaller fighter's *kup* strike moving in to hit the larger fighter's face. This is an illustration of the way White Crane hand techniques can be coherently mixed with Wing Chun kung-fu.

96. The White Crane *dang*, or double downward back-fist, is then launched against the opponent.

97. Suppose that the larger fighter weathers the previous attack and now moves in to deliver a straight punch. The smaller fighter retreats, using the distance to neutralize the punch, and prepares to deliver the White Crane *bin*, or double horizontal back-fist.

98

99

100

98. The long-range back-fist connects. This is an example of the kung-fu maxim: "Use circular force to destroy straight force; use straight force to destroy circular force."

99. Then the eyes of the opponent are attacked by the White Crane claw-hand, *jow*, whilst the opponent is caught in a Wing Chun hand-trap.

100. Finally, the larger fighter is struck with the White Crane hook punch, *chow*. Against the taller fighter, the hook punch is used in an overhand low-to-high fashion.

Conclusion

This second volume of the three-volume series on Wing Chun kung-fu comprises a concise scientific foundation for the combat art. The first volume in this series discussed and illustrated the forms of the system, the combative building blocks of the art. The three forms— *Sil Lum Tao, Chum Kil,* and *Bil Jee*—were scientifically and critically analyzed. I have set myself the requirement in these volumes of departing from the traditional constraints of secrecy and mysticism often associated, rightly or wrongly, with Chinese kung-fu. These two volumes have put the Wing Chun system under the microscope after it has been analytically dissected and the functional interrelationships between its parts examined. I have looked at a martial-art system as though it were a machine, examining each of the parts, noting strengths and weakness, and studying how the parts fit together to form a dynamic whole.

This book, concerned with the fighting skills of Wing Chun kung-fu, has continued to elaborate upon this theme. An attempt was made to understand the theory, meaning, and practical application of sticky-hand fighting, sticky-leg fighting, *chin-na,* and the theory of vital strikes to the weak points of human anatomy *(dar mak)*. This knowledge presents the Wing Chun student with a comprehensive and unified theory of combat. Traditionalists would have been content to stop at this point. Consistent though with the scientific mentality, an attempt was also made to analyze the weaknesses of the Wing Chun system with a view to discovering how a Wing Chun fighter may be defeated. Having done this, an effort was then made to show how certain parts of other martial-arts systems could be added to the Wing Chun system to enrich it, so as to produce a coherent, functional, and *complete* martial art. These remarks should not, however, be taken to imply that the fighting skills of any particular existing Wing Chun Master are inadequate, ineffective, or inferior. My concern in all three books is with the philosophical and scientific foundations of Wing Chun kung-fu, not with questions of politics. Indeed, the internal strife of the Wing Chun circle has in the past sadly lowered the status of Wing Chun kung-fu in the martial-arts world. One can, however, critically analyze a theory of the martial arts without critically analyzing martial-arts experts or theorists.

These two volumes present an outline of the empty-hand component of the Wing Chun system. The third and final volume in this series examines the Wing Chun weapons and advanced techniques. This so-called advanced knowledge is associated with the wooden-dummy form. The Wing Chun weapons include the double butterfly knives and the six-and-a-half pole set. An examination of this will complete my analysis of the Wing Chun system.

Glossary

bil jee One of the most useful hand strikes in Wing Chun, it is featured in the set form of the same name (*see next entry*).

Bil Jee The thrusting-fingers form, which was traditionally taught only to the most trusted students.

bin The White Crane kung-fu double horizontal back-fist, used to simultaneously attack two foes.

bong sao One of the most important hand movements in Wing Chun; a bent-elbow hand formation, such that the blade of the hand faces upward.

chan A philosophical concept from White Crane kung-fu, expressing the martial spirit of ruthlessness or the spiritual determination to survive combat. As the Western philosopher Nietzsche has observed: "That which does not kill me, makes me stronger." (Friedrich Nietzsche, *The Twilight of the Idols*)

chi (Pek: *ch'i, qi*) Actually meaning breath, *chi* is used to describe the intrinsic psycho-physical energy used in the internal arts.

chicken-wing bong sao This is a low *bong sao* found in the *Chum Kil* form, where the arm is held by one's side, about six inches from the body, the blade of the hand facing away from the body like a chicken's wing. It is used in *chin-na* as a lever to attack the shoulder joint.

chi gerk Wing Chun's sticky-leg attacks.

Chi Kung (Pek: *ch'i kung, qigong*) A type of training to obtain an inner harmony of the body and spirit. It is becoming well-known in the West as a method to develop one's internal psychic energy.

chil ying The name of the well-known, front-facing fighting position, in which the fighter stands in parallel stance (*see kim nur mar*).

chin The White Crane kung-fu straight punch, a powerful long-range punch executed with body rotation to add power to the punch.

chin-na The grappling moves of Wing Chun.

chi sao The Wing Chun sticky-hand techniques.

chock (Thai) The straight jab punch of Thai kickboxing.

chow The horizontal hooking punch of White Crane kung-fu.

chuan A philosophical concept from White Crane kung-fu, meaning penetration, the ability to set up an opponent and to defeat him by skillful timing.

Chum Kil The bridging the gap form of Wing Chun, which introduces three kicks into the Wing Chun system.

dang The White Crane kung-fu double downward back-fist, used to attack two opponents simultaneously from high to low.

dar mak Strikes, rather than touches, to the vital points of human anatomy, typically the acupuncture points. Contrast with *dim mak* by the degree of force employed.

dim mak The controversial theory of the poison or death touch, which according to Chinese traditional martial arts enables delayed killing of a person to occur merely by touching certain acupuncture points.

ding An upward-lifting wrist movement used in Wing Chun, not so much as a block but to open up an opponent's guard.

dit dat jow A herbal medicine whose name means warm-strike-wine, which is used to prevent arthritis, to heal bruises, to toughen the skin of striking surfaces, and to relieve the pain that results either from over-training or from sustaining a contact injury.

djab ko (Thai) Grappling moves in Thai kickboxing.

fook sao The hooking, lying-on-top hand typically used to redirect attacks.

Futshan Pai A Wing Chun association located in mainland China, in Futshan, where Wing Chun was originated in the eighteenth century by a nun and herbal physician named Ng Mui. The name is now also used to describe the style taught in Futshan.

gaun sao A Wing Chun cross-arm block that completely protects the upper body.

ging (ching) Inch-force; an immense inner power that can be utilized against an opponent at close range for an explosive shock-wave effect.

gum sao A Wing Chun push-down block that pushes an opponent's kick away from the body.

haun sao A wrist-rotating movement, used to twist around guards, or to open up a guard.

jow The clawing hand of White Crane kung-fu, used to tear and rip.

jut sao A sudden downward jerk with the edge of the heel of the hand, to clear a pathway for a strike.

kim nur mar The Wing Chun parallel stance, in which the fighter stands such that both knees and toes point inward toward the median axis of the body.

kung Extraordinary intrinsic force that can be tapped into and used after proper development through years of intense kung-fu (*chi kung*) training.

kung-fu Originally a Chinese term that meant simply an intense concentration of energy. Later, through popularization of the styles, it came to be synonymous with Chinese martial arts, especially those of the Shaolin lineage.

kup The White Crane kung-fu overhead strike, using the sharp second knuckles of the fist.

la The drawing-down hand of Wing Chun.

mat aat (Thai) The upper-cut of Thai kickboxing.

mat tong (Thai) The hook punch of Thai kickboxing.

Muay Thai Thai kick-boxing.

Pak Hok Kuen White Crane kung-fu. Originated by the monk Adato (born A.D. 1426), it is a highly developed martial-art system, employing generally big circle techniques of powerful kicks and long arm strikes.

pak sao A defensive parry.

par toi A kick from the sticky-leg (*chi gerk*) skills, using the bottom of the foot (especially the heel) to either uproot an opponent by sweeping, or to injure the lower leg, especially the ankle.

pow The White Crane kung-fu throwing punch or long range upper-cut, contacting with the sharp second knuckles of the fist to soft areas of the body such as the testicles, kidneys, or throat.

sawk (Thai) Elbow strike of Thai kickboxing.

shan A philosopical concept from White Crane kung-fu, meaning evasiveness, the capacity to avoid attacks by defensive footwork rather than blocking, then immediately counter-attacking.

Sil Lum Tao The first form of the Wing Chun system, the name means the Way of the Small Thought. (It is sometimes seen written as *Shil Lim Tao*.)

som kwok bo The correct fighting stance of Wing Chun, a side-on pose with the forward foot turned slightly in and the back foot held at 45 degrees to the median line of the body.

Sun Tzu Kuen A new syncretic style name after the great Chinese military thinker Sun Tzu, author of *The Art of War*. It combines Wing Chun, White Crane kung-fu and Thai kickboxing into a unified whole in an attempt to enrich the Wing Chun system.

tai otoshi (Japanese) The basic drop throw of judo.

t'an-tien (Cant: *tandim*) According to traditional Chinese theory, an area of the body located about three inches beneath the navel and another two inches within the body; the psychic or energy center akin to a Yogic chakra, which produces and stores the vital energy (*chi*) of the body. This energy can be directed against an opponent with the proper training.

taun sao The asking-hand of Wing Chun, a straight thrusting hand-move used to deflect punches.

te (Thai) The crocodile-tail kick or roundhouse kick of Thai kickboxing.

til sao A defensive lifting deflection designed for counter-attacking a punch with a grappling hand move.

til toi This is a very low kick used in sticky-leg (*chi gerk*) fighting, which involves striking with the shin against the soft calf muscle of the opponent's leg.

tor sao The Wing Chun *tor sao* is really a modified *fook sao* with the fingers facing downward.

tsieh A philsophical concept from White Crane kung-fu, meaning to intercept in either a soft fashion by evasive footwork, or in a hard fashion by attacking the opponent's own weapons, his arms and legs.

ukemi (Japanese) The art of falling; how to break a fall and rise uninjured.

Wing Chun/Wing Tsun A non-traditional Chinese martial art that is highly regarded as an effective self-defense system. It is said to have been invented by a nun named Ng Mui, one of the only five survivors of the total destruction of the original Shaolin Temple. Legend has it that Ng Mui traveled to Futshan province, where she developed her own fighting style and passed it on to her best disciple, the daughter of another student, bean-curd maker Yim San Sohk, whose given name was Wing Chun (Beautiful Spring).

wu sao A defensive hand move known as worshiping the Buddha.

yin/yang According to Chinese cosmology, the two basic principles of the universe, which are both opposite to each other but complementary at the same time. Yang is characterised by things that are positive, active, and male; yin, by things that are negative, passive, and female.

Ying Jow Pai Eagle Claw kung-fu.